Key Sta

SCIENCE

Homework Book

Authors - John Seaman and Richard Phillips
Series Editor - Alwyn Morgan

Letts
EDUCATIONAL

Acknowledgements

This publication is dedicated to all parents who try to help their children with their homework, and all of those who might not necessarily seek to help, but still care dearly about their children's education.

I would also like to express my thanks to the authors for responding so well to the challenge of producing these materials, and Letts Educational for their vision and commitment in promoting the role of parents in their children's education.

Finally, I would like to thank my wife, Carole, for her support, encouragement and patience.

Alwyn Morgan

First published 1998

Letts Educational, Schools and Colleges Division, 9-15 Aldine Street, London W12 8AW
Tel: 0181 740 2270, Fax: 0181 740 2280

Design by Tessa Barwick and Dave Glover

Project Management Rosine Faucompré

British Library Cataloguing-in-Publication Data

A CIP record for this book is available from the British Library

ISBN 1 84085 016 7

Printed in Great Britain by Bath Press Ltd

Letts Educational is the trading name of BPP (Letts Educational) Ltd

CONTENTS

1 ~ What are the Letts Science Homework activities for?

How can we help our children?

With these activities you can help your child in lots of ways:

1 Read through all parts of the activity together.
You could ask them to read it to you, or the other way around.

2 Help them research things they don't know.
This could be using textbooks in the home (like a children's medical handbook), going to a library, asking a friend or neighbour, or using a CD ROM or the Internet.

3 Use your family's knowledge to help with the 'Ask the family' activity.
You could ask a family friend if you don't know, or even find out together.

4 You could help to provide materials like newspapers, magazines, glue, scissors etc.

5 You could read or look at the finished homework together. You could listen while the homework is read back to you.

6 For some homeworks, if this is possible, you could visit the school to talk about your experience or knowledge and skills.

7 Be encouraging! Try to help, even if your child finds the homework difficult to understand. Be patient when they get stuck. Ring the school or get your child to ask the Science teacher for help if you all find the activities challenging!

Providing the right environment for homework

Always try to find somewhere quiet, without distractions from TV or music. Most people work best doing one thing at a time. It is usually best to get into a habit of doing homework at the same time every evening. Early in the evening is generally better, before any television or computer games or going out. Try to work together where you can easily get hold of materials and information you need. Try not to do too much of the homework for your children – encourage them to find out information independently too! Try to build their confidence and independence with your contribution to the 'Ask the family' section.

2 ~ What does each part of the homework mean?

Aim

This tells you the knowledge, understanding and skills the homework will develop if the activities are carried out carefully. Your Science teacher may only pick out parts of the homework to do, so not all the aims may apply.

National Curriculum

This tells you which part of the Science National Curriculum the homework fits into. The homework activity should be part of a carefully constructed course your children are following at school. Like any homework, it will be much more valuable if students have been carefully developing ideas at school first.

Background

This gives information for both student and family members to help prepare for the homework activities.

Homework activities

These are the part of the homework for your child to do themselves, but it might help if you read this and think through ideas together. You can help them work out what to do as you might with ordinary homework. You should certainly read their work for this part before you start the 'Ask the family' activity. Some parts of some homework activities are harder than others – your Science teacher should give guidance on which parts to do. The tasks generally get harder as you work through the homework activity.

'Ask the family' activities

This part always needs some help from someone at home, although it could be a friend or neighbour. The amount of help required varies considerably. Sometimes it may need only a few minutes, with others it might involve quite a bit of work on the part of the helper. We are sure that both students and family members will enjoy these activities and benefit from this direct contribution to education.

3 ~ Parents' and students' guide to the Science National Curriculum

Key Stage 3 covers years 7 to 9 in secondary school, usually from the ages of 11-14.

The Key Stage 3 section of the Science National Curriculum can be read in the 'National Curriculum' booklet.

You can buy this booklet from the HMSO Publications Centre (PO Box 276, London SW8 5DT), or HMSO bookshops or agents (see 'Yellow Pages' for details).

The Key Stage 3 Science National Curriculum is divided into four parts.

We have tried to explain these four parts in everyday language, but if you get stuck there is a glossary or list of useful scientific words at the end of the booklet.

- ***Experimental and Investigative Science (Sc1)***

  Students are taught how to do experiments and how to investigate like a real scientist might do.

  They have to be able to plan investigations of their own: using scientific knowledge; choosing apparatus; planning how to find the right measurements and observations and making it a fair test.

  They have to collect evidence. They should learn to use apparatus safely and skilfully. They should collect detailed measurements and observations, good enough for the job, and record them clearly in tables.

  They should be able to analyse their results; draw suitable graphs of their results, and look for patterns; draw conclusions, and explain them using ideas they have learned in Science.

They should be able to consider the strength of their evidence. Have they enough evidence? How could they improve their investigation?

- ## *Life processes and living things (Sc2)*

This is divided into five sections:

1 **Life processes and cells.**
Plants and animals have special life processes such as growth and reproduction. They are made up of parts called organs, and they in turn are made of cells. The jobs of cells and parts of cells. The jobs of certain special cells like sperm and egg cells.

2 **Humans as organisms (living things).**
The way that the body works and keeps itself alive. Feeding, the blood system, how we move, reproduction, breathing, getting energy from food, and health.

3 **Green plants.**
How plants make their food and the food for the planet. How plants get what they need to be the planet's food-factories. How plants reproduce. How plants get energy from their food once they have made it.

4 **Sorting living things, differences and their inheritance.**
Sorting animals, plants and other living things into groups. Using 'keys' to identify living things. Understanding that differences between living things of the same species can be inherited or caused by the environment. How animals and plants have been bred for certain jobs.

5 **Environments.**
How living things must suit their environment very well if they are to survive. Food chains. Ways of showing the numbers and weight of living things at each level in a food chain. How to link food chains into webs. How poisons build up in food chains. Competition in the world of living things.

- ## *Materials and their properties (Sc3)*

This is divided into three sections:

1 **Classifying materials (sorting them into groups).**
The differences between solids, liquids and gases. How the particles that make them up fit together and move differently. Using these ideas to explain physical changes in materials. What an element is and how symbols are used to represent them. Patterns of elements called the periodic table. How elements are joined up into compounds. How to separate mixtures like oil and sea water. The differences between metals and non metals.

2 **Changing materials.**
The details of physical changes like melting and dissolving, and how to explain them. Expanding and contracting. Types of rock and how they slowly change from one type to the other. Different sorts of chemical reactions. Where new materials are made. Useful new chemicals that can be made by humans. The problems of unwanted chemical reactions like rusting or rotting. Energy released by certain kinds of chemical reactions like burning fuels. Problems caused by burning fuels.

3 **Patterns in the reactions of chemicals.**
How metals react with oxygen, water and air. A metals league table of reactivity. Predicting how a metal will react. Acids and their opposites, alkalis (bases). Measuring the strengths of acids and alkalis. What acids can do to other chemicals. Understanding about how to use acids and alkalis. The problems caused by acid rain and how we could solve them.

• *Physical processes (Sc4)*

This is divided into three parts:

1 **Electricity and magnetism.**
Static electricity and its effect. What an electric current can do, and how to measure it. Different types of electric circuits and components you can put in them. The special force field around magnets. Electric magnets and their uses in bells, buzzers, central locking in cars, and loudspeakers.

2 **Forces and movement.**
Speed and how to measure it. Balanced pairs of forces (e.g. floating) and unbalanced forces (e.g. sinking). Friction and air resistance. Pivots and levers and how they can make useful tools and machines. How to work out how much advantage a simple machine gives you. Air pressure, water and liquid pressure. Explaining things using ideas of pressure. Working out pressure from your own measurements.

3 **Light and sound.**
How light travels through space. How we see things. Mirrors and lenses and how they affect light. Coloured light and spectrums (e.g. a rainbow). Sound and how it travels. Hearing and how our ears and animals' ears work. Loud and quiet, high and low sounds. Explaining sounds with shapes of sound waves.

Throughout each of these four parts of the Science National Curriculum schools have five other requirements to take into account when designing a Science course for students.

These five requirements are explained below:

1 **Systematic Enquiry**
Students should do practical and investigative work. They should use their own experience, books, CD ROMs and the Internet or other students' measurements to find things out.

2 **Application of Science**
To relate Science to everyday things. To consider the science of health and how we can improve people's lives. Understanding the science of caring for living things and the environment. To understand both the benefits and problems that Science can bring.

3 **The Nature of Scientific Ideas**
How scientific theories have changed and developed. How evidence is important to Science. How Science has affected and been affected by society and history.

4 **Communication**
To use scientific words, symbols and units. To show their ideas using diagrams, charts, tables and graphs in a scientific and mathematical way.

5 **Health and Safety**
To learn to recognise hazards in their practical work. To use information to assess the risks involved in practical work before they do it. To control the risks to themselves and others

In conclusion, family support can make a difference to any student's learning. We hope that these materials will provide all members of the family with the opportunity to increase their knowledge and understanding of Science.

EGGSACTLY RIGHT FOR THE JOB

Aims:

~To find out how some human body cells are designed for special jobs~

~To study a giant cell from another animal and find out the job of each part of this cell~

National Curriculum:

~Sc2 Life & Living processes 1e: Life processes and cell activity~

Background

~All living things are made up of cells. Cells are usually so small that they can only be seen with a microscope.~

~Your body is made of special cells with special jobs (or functions), for example, nerve cells are very long and thin like wires for carrying messages through your body.~

Homework Activity - Ask the family

Find out about how these cells in your body are special using a library, book or CD ROM or by asking someone at home or a neighbour.

SPECIAL CELL	WHAT IS ITS JOB?	HOW IS IT SUITED TO ITS SPECIAL JOB?
Sperm cell		
Nerve cell		
Muscle cell		
White blood cell		
Red blood cell		

Ask someone at home to help you research these tasks:

1 A chicken's egg is a giant special cell. Crack open a raw egg into a bowl or glass. Look carefully at the egg and its shell. This egg will probably not have been fertilised by a male chicken.

2 Think what special jobs an egg must do after it has been fertilised.

3 Look again at the broken egg. What is the name of each part of the egg? How does each part help a baby chicken to survive?

CAN THAT ORGAN PLAY A TUNE?

Homework Activity

1 Name as many human body organs as you can.

2 The organs in this picture are jumbled up. Match each one to its correct function (job) and write the correct numbers and letters down.

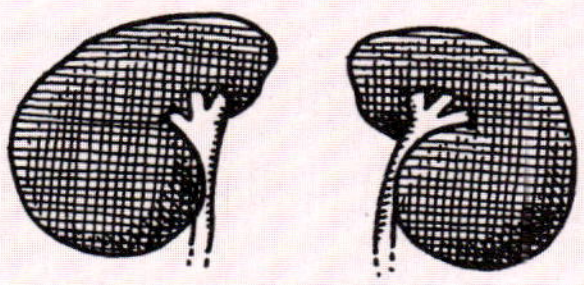

A KIDNEYS
1 Getting food into your blood.

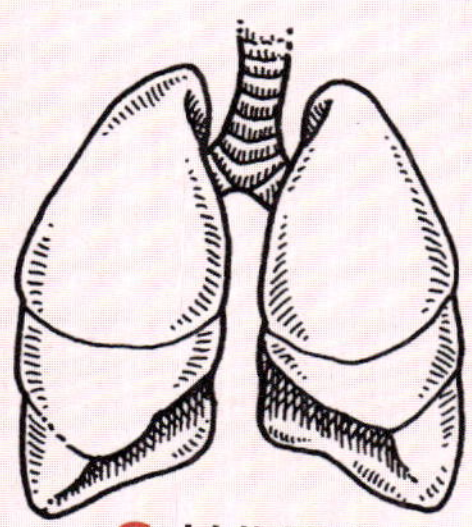

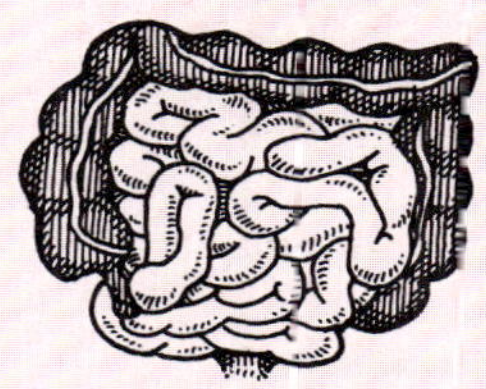

B INTESTINES
2 Storing information

C LUNGS
3 Making blood cells

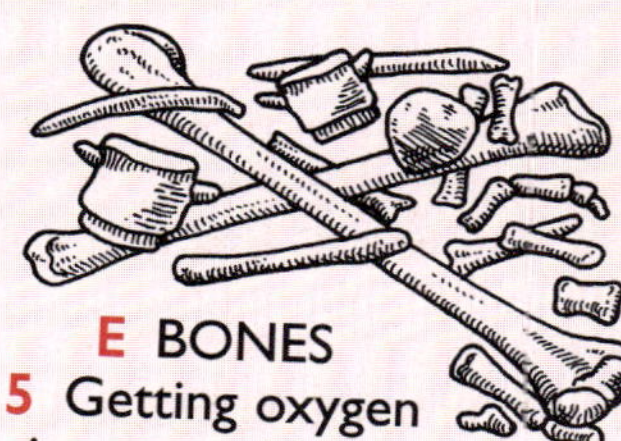

E BONES
5 Getting oxygen into your blood

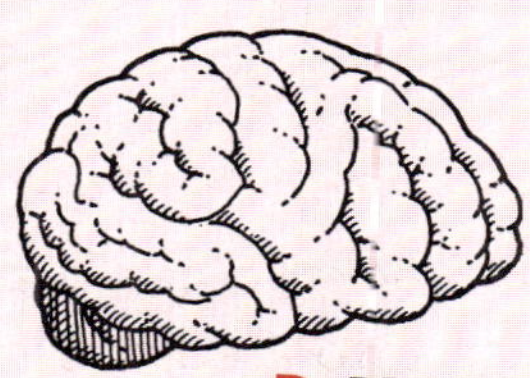

D BRAIN
4 Making urine

~ Ask the family ~

Can you match these diseases to the organs they affect? Copy out the table first. You will need to ask for help.

DISEASE	ORGANS
Rickets	
Cardiac arrest	
Ulcers	
Cystic fibrosis	
Meningitis	
Cystitis	

Aims:

~To match jobs (or functions) to particular organs~

~To become aware of the jobs of organs through a family activity about diseases and the organs they affect~

National Curriculum:

~Sc2 Life & Living processes 1a: Life processes~

Background:

~An organ is a collection of different cells arranged to do a special job, or more than one job.~

~Scientists use the word 'function' instead of 'job'.~

THE RIGHT FOOD FOR THE JOB?

Aims:

~To understand the jobs of different types of food~

~To offer advice on improving problem diets~

National Curriculum:

~Sc2 Life & Living processes 2c: Nutrition~

Background:

~Fatty foods give you energy and help to keep you warm, but too much is bad for you and can cause heart disease.~

~Starchy foods and sweet foods (carbohydrates) give you energy. You should eat some every day, but less if you do not get much exercise because any food not used up will be turned into fat.~

Homework Activity

Making a Food Collage

Collect as many pictures of food as you can from old newspapers and magazines. Colour pictures will look better. Put the pictures of food into three groups:

Food for Energy

Food for Body Building and Repairing your body

Food that adds vitamins

Stick the pictures down in an attractive way (keeping them in the three groups).

Add a colourful title and any explanations you think will improve your collage.

THE RIGHT FOOD FOR THE JOB?

~ Ask the family ~

Imagine you are an 'agony aunt' or 'agony uncle'. Ask someone to help you write replies to these diet problem letters:

Dr Doctor ...

Dear Doctor,
I am sixteen. I am really thin because I think it looks good. Whenever I do any exercise I feel really tired and I often feel weak just before meals. I try not to eat much and I only eat 'diet' foods. Can you help me?

Yours, Cynthia T.

Dear Doctor,
I live in a small village. My family are quite poor. My legs have not grown very straight and I want to help my brothers and sisters avoid the same problem. What sort of food am I missing and what should my family try to eat?

Yours, Susan D.

Dear Doctor,
I have a real weight problem, and my skin is spotty too. I really like sport but I don't like taking my clothes off in the shower. I like chips and chocolate. I don't like vegetables. What can I do?

Yours, Frank D.

Dear Doctor,
I am a long distance runner. I try not to eat much the day before a race because I feel nervous. I often get really tired even though I am very fit. What do you suggest?

Yours, Ranjit S.

Background:

~Meat, fish, beans, milk and nuts are good for repairing your body and building it up when you are growing. These foods contain plenty of protein.~

~Some foods help you to stay healthy. Vitamins and minerals that help you stay healthy are found in fresh fruit and vegetables, dairy foods, fish and meat.~

BALANCING YOUR FOOD

Aims:

~To understand what makes a balanced diet~

~To recognise the foods that make up a balanced diet~

National Curriculum:

~Sc2 Life & Living processes 2d: Nutrition~

Background:

~A balanced diet is made up of the right types of food in the correct amounts.~

~Many recent surveys suggest that pupils in schools eat too many fat and meat products and too few vegetables. This diet could make British children unhealthy.~

Homework Activity

TYPE OF FOOD	AMOUNT YOU NEED	SOURCES (WHERE YOU GET THESE FOOD TYPES FROM)
Carbohydrate 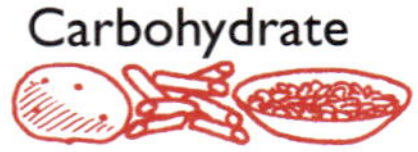	Some every day (more when active)	Starchy foods e.g. potato, pasta, plantain, rice, cereals
Protein 	Some every day (more when growing)	Meat, fish, pulses or beans, nuts, milk, cheese, eggs
Fats 	A little (more when growing)	Meat, butter, margarine, cheese, vegetable oil, eggs, nuts
Minerals (Iron & Calcium) 	Small amounts regularly	Iron in fresh fruit, vegetables, and liver. Calcium in cheese, milk and yoghurt
Vitamins 	Small amounts regularly	Fresh fruit and vegetables, liver, milk and cheese
Fibre 	A fair amount regularly	Brown rice, brown bread, cereals containing bran, and fruit and vegetables

1 Write down the menu on sale at your school one day this week.

2 Pick out from the menu a balanced diet selection for one lunch.

3 Design a leaflet or poster that would encourage new pupils at your school to eat a balanced diet every day.

Use the information in the table above to help you. Make the poster clear and eye catching – a good picture always catches people's attention. Use clear, big, bold writing.

~ Ask the family ~

Ask one member of your family to describe their diet for this week. If necessary, suggest how they might improve their diet by cutting down on some foods and eating more of others. Write an advice letter to her/him as if you were writing in a health magazine.

FILLING WELL?

Homework Activity

1 Go to the dentist, doctor or clinic (ask for permission or go with an adult). Collect some leaflets and posters on:

how to brush your teeth properly

the foods that are good for your teeth

how to use dental floss

2 Design a poster for the bedroom or playroom of a young child that will show them how to care for their teeth.

Make it bold, colourful and clear using simple words because a small child may not be able to read well.

~ Ask the family ~

Ask someone at home to help you do this research. You will need to use a mirror.

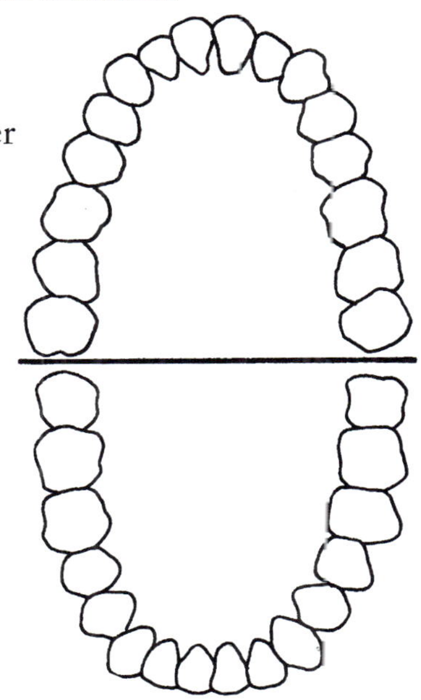

1 Use the diagram to make a map of your teeth. Map the teeth of an older family member next to your own.

Your teacher may give you a bigger version of this diagram to use.

2 Put a cross over each tooth that is not there, like this: ☒

Draw each filling on the tooth like this: ●

3 Try to find out why children today have far fewer fillings than children 30 years ago.

Aims:

~To find out the best way to care for your teeth~

~To find out why people generally have much healthier teeth than their parents~

~To map your own teeth and the teeth of a family member~

National Curriculum:

~AT 2 reading: Range of Sc2 Life & Living processes 2d: Nutrition~

Background:

~Tooth decay is caused by acid made by bacteria (germs) growing on food stuck to your teeth and gums.~

~This acid dissolves the hard outer part (enamel) of your teeth.~

~Cleaning your teeth and gums regularly and properly removes the food and germs from your teeth and gums.~

GIVE YOUR WHITES THE CLOSE-UP TEST

Aims:

~To plan an investigation to compare a biological washing powder with a non-biological washing powder~

~To carry out your investigation at home~

~To understand how enzymes help us digest our food~

National Curriculum:

~Sc2 Life & Living processes 2d: Nutrition Sc1 Investigating~

Background:

~Enzymes are special chemicals that living things use to digest (break down) their food, e.g. your spit contains enzymes that start to digest starch.~

~Biological washing powders contain enzymes to break down stains.~

Homework Activity

Design a fair test to compare a biological washing powder with a non-biological one. You are going to see for yourself which one washes whiter.

Make sure you can do the test at home.

Remember all that you have been taught about a fair test.

Your teacher may help you to plan your investigation.

~ Ask the family ~

1 Ask permission before you carry out your plan. Ask someone at home to help you.

You might be able to use a washing machine, but hand-washing in a sink will be fine. Choose a few small items or things such as tea-towels or handkerchieves. It is easier to see whether light colours are clean – white is easiest of all.

2 Write a report on what you found out.

YOUR HEART SURVIVAL KIT

Homework Activity

You will need to research these questions by asking family members, or using CD ROMs or home medical reference books.

1 Find out what is wrong with a person's blood system if they have the following diseases or conditions:

Anaemia	**High blood pressure**
Hole-in-the-Heart	**Leukaemia**
Heart attack	**Haemophilia**

2 Can you find out how one of these diseases or conditions is treated (made better)?

~ Ask the family ~

1 Ask someone at home to tell you about the best ways to keep your heart healthy.

Think about:

- lifestyle
- exercise
- what you eat and drink
- smoking and passive smoking.

2 Fact: Most people in this country die from some kind of heart disease! Design a leaflet (using folded plain A4 paper) called your HEART SURVIVAL KIT which explains how to keep your heart healthy and fit throughout your life, starting when you are young. Make it funny, easy to read and colourful. Grab people's attention with a gripping cover!

Aims:

~To understand how our blood system works~

~To find out about heart disease~

National Curriculum:

~Sc2 Life & Living processes 2f: Circulation~

Background:

~Your blood is a liquid that carries food, oxygen, waste and many other things around your body.~

~Your blood helps you fight disease, and it can block any leaks by itself.~

~Your heart is a pump that pushes the blood around.~

~Blood travels in pipes called arteries and veins, and tiny tubes called capillaries.~

BAD BLOOD?

Aims:

~To understand some of the jobs of parts of the blood by finding out what happens when things go wrong~

~To research the treatment of blood disease~

National Curriculum:

~Sc2 Life & Living processes 2f: Circulation~

Background:

Your blood is made of:

~Plasma – a liquid that carries food, waste, heat, hormones and other things around your body.~

~Red blood cells that carry oxygen.~

~White blood cells that help to fight disease.~

~Platelets, which are tiny particles that help blood to clot.~

Homework Activity

You may need to ask for help from someone at home or look in a medical book or CD ROM.

Find out what is wrong with a person's blood if they have one of these diseases:

- **Haemophilia**
- **Leukaemia**
- **Sickle-cell anaemia**

~ Ask the family ~

Ask someone at home to help you to research these tasks. Be sensitive when asking questions because some of these illnesses are serious and the person you speak to may have a close friend or relative with one of these problems.

Find out how each of the blood problems in the first part of the homework is treated or cured.

GOOD BLOOD

Homework Activity

You may need to ask for help from someone at home or look in a medical book or CD ROM.

1 How many different types of blood (blood groups) do human beings have? What are they called?

Which blood group can be given to most people?

Which blood group can take blood from most other people?

What could happen if you were given the wrong type of blood?

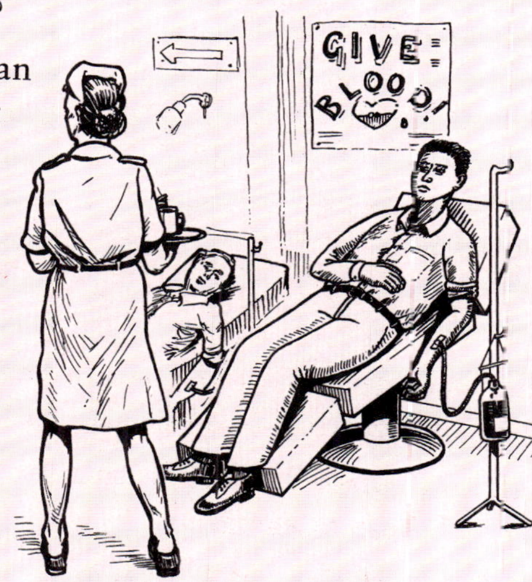

2 Find out what is different about the red blood cells in blood of different blood groups.

~ Ask the family ~

Ask someone at home to help you research these tasks.

1 Find out what blood group people in your family or friends are.

2 Find pairs of people in your family or friends who could safely give blood to each other. Make sure you are clear who would be the donor and who would be the recipient (person getting the blood).

Aims:

~To understand the reasons for blood transfusions~

~To understand there are different types of blood and that only some of them can be given safely in a blood transfusion~

~To research the difference between the cells in different blood types~

National Curriculum:

~SC2 Life & Living processes 2f: Circulation~

Background:

~When someone has had an accident or an operation they may need to replace some of the blood they have lost.~

~A blood transfusion means giving a patient someone else's blood.~

THEM BONES, THEM BONES

Aims:

~To understand the work that bones and joints do by finding out what happens when they go wrong~

~To find out how some joint and bone problems can be corrected~

~To understand how a doctor or physiotherapist may correct these problems~

National Curriculum:

~Sc2 Life and Living processes 2g: Movement~

Background:

~A physiotherapist is a person who treats muscle, bone and joint problems. You may be sent to see a physiotherapist after the doctor has worked out what the problem is.~

Homework Activity

You may need to ask someone in your family or look in a medical book or CD ROM.

1 Find out what is wrong with joints or bones in the following injuries or problems:

- **a sprain**
- **a dislocation**
- **a fracture**
- **a slipped disc**
- **arthritis**

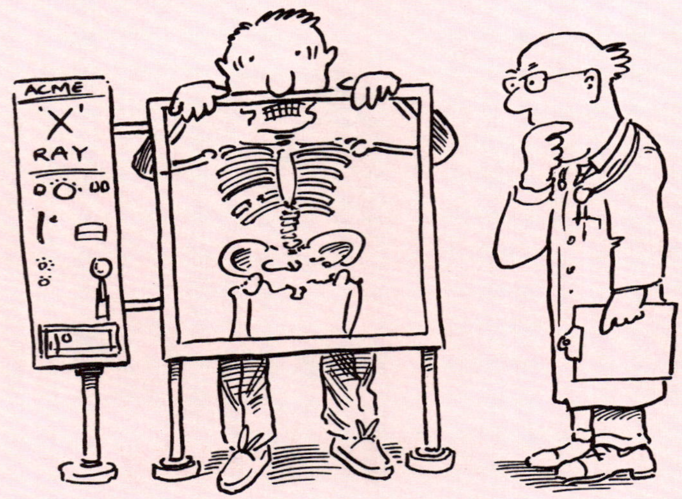

2 For each of the injuries or problems try to find out how a doctor or physiotherapist could help.

~ Ask the family ~

Find out if anyone in your family has had a joint or bone injury. Ask them to describe what happened and write down their description.

What treatment did they have to improve their injury or problem?

GERMS - A MATTER OF LIFE OR DEATH

Homework Activity

1 Make a list of all the health problems the members of your family have had.

2 Put these illnesses into two groups:
a) those that you think are caused by microbes;
b) those that are not caused by microbes.
Hint: a broken leg may be caused by falling down the stairs, not by germs.

3 Using books or a CD ROM try to find out which illnesses in group (a) are caused by a virus and which are caused by bacteria.

~ Ask the family ~

1 Find out which vaccinations you have had.

2 For each of the diseases you have been vaccinated against, ask the oldest members of your family if they know what having these diseases feels like.

3 Find out what happens when you are vaccinated.

Aims:

~ To understand that some health problems are caused by microbes and some are not ~

~ To show that the body can benefit from vaccines ~

National Curriculum:

~ Sc2 Life & Living Processes 4r,s: Health ~

Background:

~ Microbes are very small living things. You need a microscope to see them. ~

~ Bacteria and viruses are microbes that are sometimes called 'germs'. ~

~ Most microbes are harmless to us but some can make us ill or even kill us. ~

~ Being vaccinated can help to protect us from a disease caused by a microbe. ~

FOOD FACTORIES

Aims:

~To understand what green plants need to grow~

~To understand how green plants make their own food~

~To appreciate that plants increase in mass or weight as they make food and grow~

National Curriculum:

~Sc2 Life & Living processes 3a,b: Green plants as organisms~

Background:

~Plants can make their own food, using simple chemicals they take from their surroundings.~

~They use the food they make to grow into healthy plants.~

~Plants increase in size and mass (or weight) as they grow.~

Homework Activity

1 a) If you plant an acorn what will it grow into, if you are lucky?

b) What should you give the plant regularly to make sure it grows well?

c) Estimate (guess) the mass or weight of an acorn.

d) Roughly what do you think the mass (or weight) of the plant will be when it is fully grown?

e) Where has all the extra mass (or weight) come from when the plant is fully grown?

f) Why would the plant be unlikely to grow well if you put a box over it?

2 a) Complete the labels on the diagram to show the things a growing plant takes from the soil and the air around it when it is making food.

b) Show on the diagram you are given where the plant gets its energy from to make its own food.

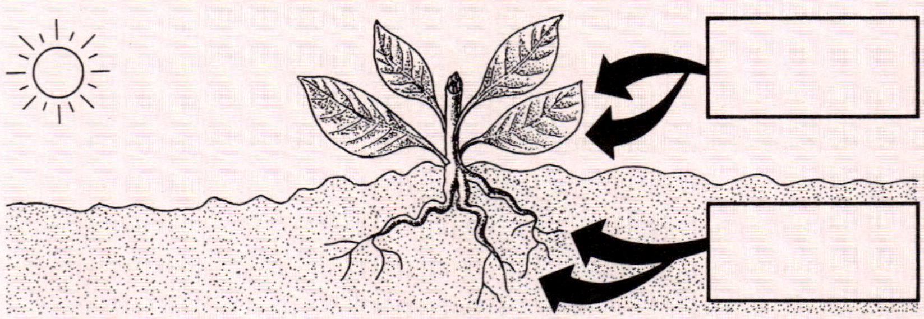

~ Ask the family ~

1 Why do goldfish swim around more actively if you bubble air through the water they live in?

2 You can put pond weed in a goldfish tank instead of bubbling air through the water. Can you explain why this helps the goldfish to be more active, particularly during the day?

CH-CH-CH-CH CHANGES

Homework Activity

1 Draw a table in your book or folder with two columns, one headed **girls,** the other headed **boys.**

Write in this table all the changes that happen to boys' and girls' bodies as they go through puberty.

Make them as sensible and realistic as you can!

You can include things they will think/feel.

2 Next to each change in your table that is a physical change put the letter 'p'.

Next to each change in your table that is an emotional change put an 'e'.

~ Ask the family ~

Ask someone at home to help you with this activity. It may sometimes be hard for older people to talk about sex because of the way they were brought up. Make sure that the person you ask is not embarrassed by your questions.

1 Imagine you are a teenager suffering from some emotional problems at home or school during puberty.

Write a short problem page letter to a teen magazine describing these problems.

2 Now imagine you are the magazine problem-solver and write a reply to your own letter. You do not have to show this work to your teacher if you do not wish to.

Aims:

~To recall the changes that happen to boys and girls during puberty~

~To understand the difference between physical and emotional changes during puberty~

~To consider the difficulties that emotional changes can sometimes bring for teenagers~

National Curriculum:

~Sc2 Life & Living processes 2j: Reproduction~

Background:

~This homework will follow lessons about sex organs, puberty and periods.~

~A physical change during puberty is a change in the body of a girl or boy that prepares them for being parents in the future.~

~An emotional change during puberty is a change in your behaviour or the way you feel in your mind.~

Aims:

~To understand why periods happen~

~To understand some of the physical and emotional changes that take place during puberty~

National Curriculum:

~Sc2 Life & Living processes 2j: Reproduction~

Homework Activity

How much can you remember from your classwork? If you have forgotten, ask at home or read your classwork again.

1 Answer these questions in sentences:

How often does a girl or woman have a period?

What happens inside the womb every month?

What causes the womb to bleed each month?

What happens to periods if a girl or a woman becomes pregnant? Why does this happen?

2 A girl is born with all the eggs she will have in her life. They begin to ripen at puberty and are released once a month after her periods start.

Find out roughly when a girl's periods may start when a woman's periods stop. These ages can be very different for different girls and women. Try to work out how many eggs a baby girl has when she is born.

~ Ask the family ~

Ask someone at home to help you with this activity. It may sometimes be hard for older people to talk about sex because of the way they were brought up. Make sure that the person you ask is not embarrassed by your questions.

Write your answers to these questions as an article for a magazine!

1 At what age can a person still be a mother or a father?

2 Why is this age different for men and women?

3 What does menopause mean and at what age does it usually happen?

4 Just like puberty, menopause can cause some emotional difficulties. How might that person feel?

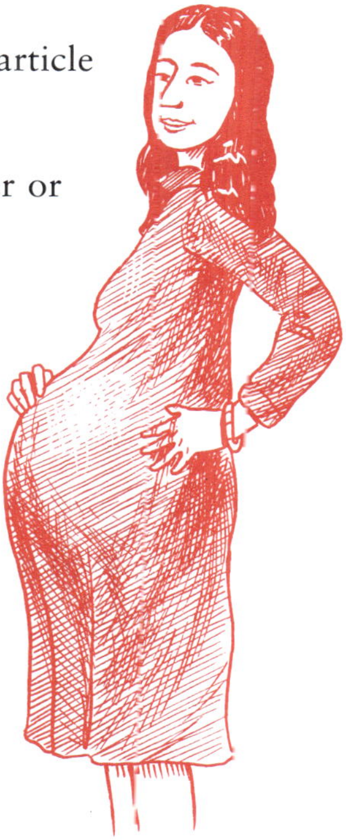

Background:

~This homework will follow lessons about sex organs, puberty and periods.~

~Sperm cells are made in the testes of boys and egg cells are made in the ovaries of girls after puberty. The age of puberty is different for everyone. It is roughly 11-15 in girls and 12-16 in boys.~

~After puberty the bodies of boys and girls change and become able to have babies. Girls start to release eggs and have periods, boys start to make sperm.~

~If a boy and girl past puberty have sex, the girl can become pregnant unless contraceptives (such as condoms) are used.~

BABY FOOD

Aims:

~To understand the position and job of the womb (uterus) in looking after a growing baby~

~To understand how the baby is fed and protected and how it gets rid of its waste~

National Curriculum:

~Sc2 Life & Living processes 2k: Reproduction~

Background:

~A baby grows inside its mother's womb (or uterus) in the lower part of her belly. It is about the size of a fist when she is not pregnant. The uterus stretches as the baby grows. It is a muscular bag which can push the baby out when it is ready to be born.~

Homework Activity

How much can you remember from your classwork? If you have forgotten, look up the answers.

1 Which of these statements are true and which are false?

SENTENCE	TRUE OR FALSE
If a mother smokes it has no effect on the baby.	
The mother's blood mixes with the baby's blood.	
The baby gets food and oxygen from its mother's blood.	
The mother's blood runs very close to the baby's blood.	
The baby's blood passes backwards and forwards in the cord through what will later become its belly button.	
The baby does not move around until it is born.	
The baby is protected from bumps by liquid it floats in.	
Most of the baby's waste passes into its mother's blood.	

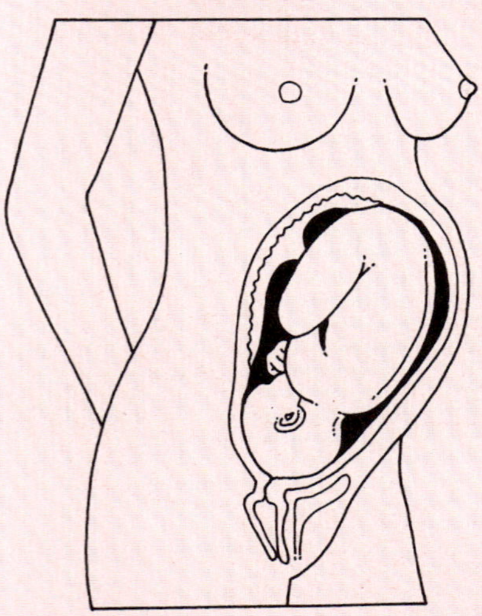

2 Where does the baby grow inside its mother?

Draw a sketch of this diagram and write in all the names of the parts around the baby that you know.

~ Ask the family ~

Ask someone at home who has had a baby or seen a baby being born to help you with these questions.

1 What comes out of the mother's womb before the baby is born?

2 What comes out of the mother's womb after the baby is born?

3 How is the baby joined to this large object and what does the doctor or nurse do to separate them shortly after the birth?

4 What is the job of this large object and what is its scientific name?

5 What is its common name?

Background:

~The baby is fed from its mother's blood and gets its oxygen from there too. It cannot breathe inside the womb because it is surrounded by liquid (fluid). All its waste goes from its blood into its mother's blood.~

~The food and oxygen are exchanged for waste in an organ called the placenta.~

~The baby is connected to the placenta by the umbilical cord. The mother's blood runs in the womb close to the placenta, but the mother's blood and the baby's blood never mix.~

DYING FOR A SMOKE

Aims:

~To understand some of the health problems that smoking can cause~

~To be aware of some of the reasons why people start smoking~

~To realise some of the problems of giving up smoking~

National Curriculum:

~Sc2 Life & Living processes 2m: Breathing~

Background:

~Cigarette smoke contains nicotine, tar, carbon monoxide and other substances.~

~Nicotine is a drug that calms people down, but it is very hard to give up.~

~Tar causes lung cancer.~

~Carbon monoxide is a gas that can damage your blood.~

Homework Activity - Ask the family

1 Collect health warnings from cigarette advertisements in newspapers and magazines. Write an explanation for each of the different warnings you found and make a poster using the cut out warnings and your own explanations.

2 Do a survey on smoking. If nobody in your family smokes, ask some neighbours or friends who do smoke. Use these questions to start and try to think of some more for yourself:

- Why did you start smoking?
- If you have given up why did you stop?
- How old were you when you started?
- How much do/did you spend each month on cigarettes?
- Would you like to give up?
- Why do you not give up?
- Do you think smoking should be banned in public places?
- Do you think advertising makes some people smoke?

3 **Smoking is increasing amongst school children.** Use the results from your survey to design a leaflet to persuade school children not to start smoking.

LEGAL DRUG ADDICTS

Homework Activity

1 Write a short story about an imaginary person who drinks too much.

Imagine the trouble they could get into and how much it would cost them.

Imagine the health problems it could cause.

Write about the difficulties their heavy drinking could cause for their family.

2 What advice would you give to someone who has a drink problem? Remember that (like any drug) it can be difficult to give up.

3 Find out about legal alcohol limits for drinking.

~ Ask the family ~

Ask someone at home to help you with these tasks. Be sensitive when interviewing people. If they do not want to help you, find someone who does.

1 Find out how much beer, wine or spirits contains a single unit of alcohol.

2 Find out the legal alcohol limit (in units) for driving a car?

3 Work out how much of each of these you can legally drink before driving: • Beer • Wine • Spirits

Aims:

~To understand that alcohol is a drug and that it affects a person's moods and behaviour~

~To understand some of the problems that drinking too much can cause for some people~

National Curriculum:

~Sc2 Life & Living processes 2q: Health~

Background:

~Alcohol is a drug. It makes a person less sensitive, and makes them react more slowly.~

~Alcohol is a legal drug taken by anyone who drinks beer, wine or spirits.~

~Many people die every year from diseases, accidents and other problems caused by drinking too much alcohol.~

A BIT SEEDY!

Aims:

~To investigate how a wide range of plants spread their seeds~

~To find out how these seeds are adapted or suited to their jobs~

National Curriculum:

~Sc2 Life & Living processes 3f: Reproduction~

Background:

~Do this activity in the late summer when there are plenty of seeds to find.~

~Plants have four main ways of spreading their seeds: Some are inside fruit for an animal to eat; some have hooks that catch in an animal's fur; some are blown by the wind; some have pods that twist as they dry, flicking the seeds out.~

Homework Activity

Seeds, fruits and berries can be poisonous so keep them somewhere safe. Keep them away from small children and do not eat any yourself.

Make a collection of different kinds of fruits, berries and seeds. You only need one or two of each kind.

Wherever you live you will find weeds or garden plants making seeds.

If the plants are in someone else's garden be sure to ask for permission.

Remember that trees also make seeds.

~ Ask the family ~

Ask someone at home to help you with this activity.

1. Put your collection of seeds, berries and fruits into the four groups below. Use the background information to help you decide where they belong.
   - eaten by animals
   - stick to animals
   - spread by wind
   - flicked out by pods
2. Draw the items you have collected in a table you have designed yourself. Ask for help when naming them.
3. Pick one from each group and explain how it is designed for its own method of travel.

GARDENERS' QUESTION TIME

Homework Activity

1 Find the names of the three chemical elements present in all chemical fertilisers. They are shown on the packet or bag by the letters N, P and K.

2 How can a garden be fertilised without using chemicals?

3 How are wild places fertilised?

~ Ask the family ~

Ask someone at home who knows about gardening to help you to answer these questions.

1 What does the term 'organic fertiliser' mean?

2 What are three advantages of using organic fertilisers? Why are they not used as much as they once were?

3 How would you make a compost bin and what would you put in it?

4 What element is needed to help plants to grow good flowers?

Which minerals are needed for good leaf growth in plants?

(Hint: Use N, P and K in your answers)

Aims:

~To know that some minerals are necessary for healthy plant growth~

~To understand the differences between chemical and organic fertilisers~

National Curriculum:

~Sc2 Life & Living processes 3d: Nutrition in green plants~

Background:

~All plants take minerals from the soil they grow in. These minerals are essential for healthy growth.~

~Extra minerals are given as fertilisers.~

~Artificial or synthetic fertilisers are made from chemicals in factories.~

~Organic fertilisers use natural waste such as compost-rotting plants or vegetable waste, or manure – the waste of plant-eating animals.~

HOW GREEN ARE YOUR FAMILY'S FINGERS?

Aims:

~To understand that plants reproduce sexually through their flowers~

~To understand that some flower parts become fruits containing seeds if they are fertilised by pollen~

~To know that it is possible to make new plants by taking cuttings~

~To share family expertise in growing new plants from seeds~

National Curriculum:

~Sc2 Life & Living Processes 3f: Plant reproduction~

Homework Activity

Ask someone at home to help you or use a library, science textbook or CD ROM.

1 What type of insects have you seen carrying pollen by accident? Try to name at least three.

2 Why do insects visit flowers?

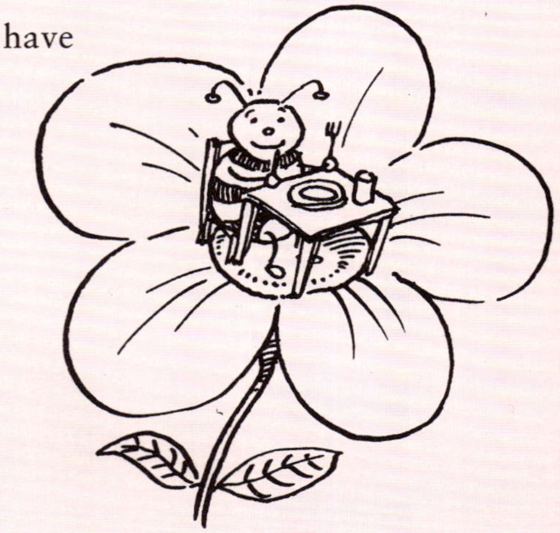

3 Find three different fruits at home or in a garden. Ask permission first and make sure they can be eaten afterwards.

Cut each one in half and draw what it looks like inside. Label the seeds, and put an arrow to show where you think the flower was.

HOW GREEN ARE YOUR FAMILY'S FINGERS?

~ Ask the family ~

Ask someone who is interested in gardening to help you to answer these questions.

1 Find the names of some plants that can be grown from seed.

2 Explain in a few sentences or draw pictures to show how to do this. Mention any special ways of making sure that most of the seeds grow.

3 An easy way to make new plants is by taking cuttings. Find out from which plants grow well from cuttings. Try to name at least three. Describe or draw how cuttings are grown.

4 What colour flowers would you expect if you grew seeds from one of your own plants?

5 What colour flowers would you expect to see on plants you have taken as cuttings?

Background:

~Flowers are the sex organs of plants. Egg cells called ovules grow in the flower's ovary. Pollen contains a male sex cell.~

~Pollen from one flower travels to the female part of another flower by using insects or the wind. Some plants use birds or bats to carry their pollen.~

~After it is fertilised, each egg cell becomes a seed.~

~The flower petals wither away but part of the flower grows into a fruit.~

KEY TO THE GARDEN

Aims:

~To devise simple keys for shapes, and for living things~

~To test one key~

National Curriculum:

~Sc2 Life & Living processes 4c: Classification~

Background:

~This homework will follow a lesson about keys at school~

~A key is a series of questions with two simple answers that lead to other questions. It can help you to identify a plant or an animal you have never seen before. ~

KEY FOR GARDEN BIRDS

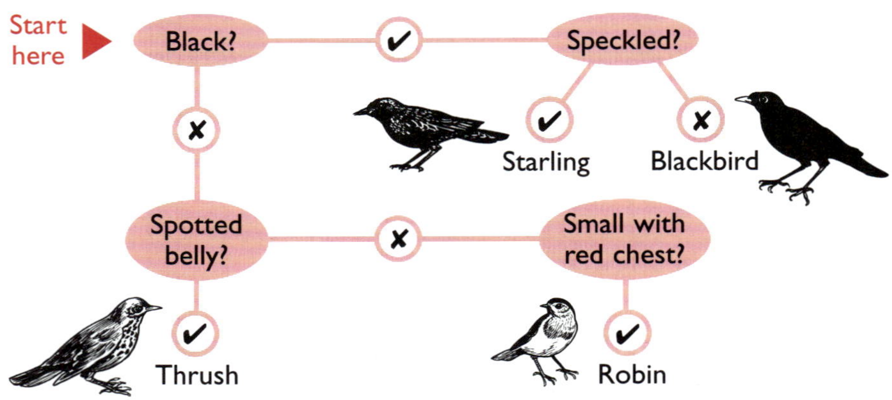

Homework Activity

You will need a large sheet of paper for this project.

The project is to design a key to teach a young child the names for shapes.

1 Draw these shapes.

2 Colour them brightly to make them attractive and interesting.

3 Add a title. Make the writing big and clear.

Include some difficult words and some easy ones so that children of different ages can use your key.

4 Try out your shapes key on some young children.

~ Ask the family ~

Ask someone at home to help you with this task.

Ask someone who knows about gardening to help you to design a key for six garden plants.

Homework Activity

1 Use this table to put pets into the correct animal groups. Try to find three pets in each group. Some of them will be unusual pets.

ANIMAL GROUP	PETS
Fish	
Amphibians	
Reptiles	
Birds	
Mammals	

~ Ask the family ~

Ask someone you know who has pets to help you to research these tasks.

1 Choose one pet from each group.

2 For each pet you choose find out whether it lays eggs or not, and how it look after its eggs or babies.

3 Fish have many different ways of caring for their young. If you can find someone who knows about fish, do a mini-project on how they care for their young.

Aims:

~To classify pet animals~

~To find out how different animals reproduce and care for their young~

National Curriculum:

~Sc2 Life & Living processes 4d: Classification~

Background:

~Fish live in water, have scales and fins, lay eggs and breathe with gills.~

~Amphibians live partly on land and partly in water, lay eggs and have moist skin which helps them to breathe.~

~Reptiles live on land, have dry scaly skin, lay eggs and breathe with lungs.~

~Birds live on land, have feathers and wings, lay eggs and breathe with lungs.~

~Mammals live mainly on land, have fur, breathe with lungs and have babies that grow in the female's body.~

ON SAFARI OUTSIDE YOUR DOOR

Aims:

~To classify living things in a garden, park or wild place~

~To produce an illustrated report on the life-forms found~

National Curriculum:

~Sc2 Life & Living processes 4d: Classification~

Background:

~There are thousands of animals living all around you. Many animals hide under leaves, in cracks in walls, under the roof, or in the soil.~

~There may be more varieties of bird visiting gardens than in many parts of the countryside.~

Homework Activity

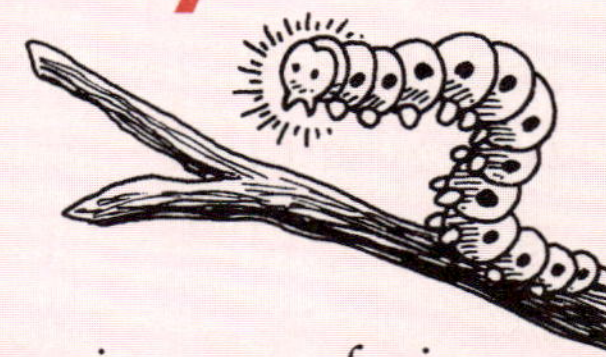

1 You are going on safari outside your own door. Like all good modern explorers you will only bring back pictures and stories, and the names of the animals you find.

Many of the animals you will find are microbeasts. You will have to search carefully for them.

Write a report on your safari. You should describe what you found and where you found it.

Draw sketches of the animals you found, or even take photos (ask permission first).

2 When you get back to school your teacher will help you to arrange the living things you found into groups.

~ Ask the family ~

Ask someone at home to help you to research these tasks.

Look up all the wildlife programmes on TV in the coming week. Choose two programmes to watch about animal life in other countries.

Keep a record of all the animals you see in these two programmes. Try to arrange these animals in their proper scientific groups.

IT'S A DOG'S LIFE

Homework Activity - Ask the family

Ask someone at home to help you to do these tasks.

1 Find the names of four different varieties of apples.

Include at least one that is used for cooking. Remember that each variety has been specially bred to look and taste the way it does.

2 Describe the colour, size, texture and taste of each apple. Put this information in a table you design yourself.

3 Find one breed of dog originally used to do each of these jobs.

JOB	BREED OF DOG
Herding sheep	
Racing	
Hunting rabbits in burrows	
Tracking animals	
Hunting wolves	
Pulling a sledge	

Aim:

~To understand that selective breeding can create new varieties of plants and animals~

National Curriculum:

~Sc2 Life & Living processes 4e: Inheritance – selective breeding~

Background:

~For thousands of years, humans have been selecting (picking out) animals and plants they wanted and mating them to produce even better breeds for a particular job.~

~All dogs are believed to have been bred from one kind of dog. They are all the same species. However, dogs have been bred for all kinds of different uses.~

A FAMILY RESEMBLANCE

Aims:

~To understand that variation or differences between people can be inherited or caused by the environment~

~To explore your own family tree for evidence of inherited and environmental differences~

National Curriculum:

~Sc2 Life & Living Processes 4b: Variation~

Homework Activity

Sort the list of human features below into three groups:

1. Inherited features;
2. Environmental features;
3. Both Inherited and Environmental features.

Put them into a table you design yourself.

Height, Intelligence, Eye colour, Tongue-rolling, Freckles, Liking pizza, Short-sightedness, Skin colour, Hair colour, Scars, Baldness in men, Colour blindness, Skill at tennis, Being artistic, Speaking with an accent, Aggressiveness.

A FAMILY RESEMBLANCE

~ Ask the family ~

1 Ask family members to help you to draw a family tree. Go as far back as you can. Don't worry if you cannot find out everyone's name. Most families are very complicated.

2 See if you can find one or two inherited features, such as hair colour or ear shape, through your family tree.

Look at the first part of the Homework Activity with family members to decide which differences are inherited and which are environmental.

3 For one generation (e.g. brothers and sisters) write down some differences that you know were caused by their environment.

Background:

~All living things show some variation. Variations between individuals of the same species are important in a constantly changing world. They help to ensure that some members of the species always survive.~

~Differences that are passed down from one generation to the next (inherited) are carried in your genes.~

~Other differences may be caused by your lifestyle and surroundings, such as diet, home, exercise, diseases and accidents. These are environmental differences. Environmental differences are not carried in your genes.~

IT'S BECOMING A HABITAT

Aims:

~To understand that each habitat contains different kinds of plants and animals that fit into the place very well~

~To match climate with plants and animals in different habitats~

~To match house plants to desert and rainforest habitats~

National Curriculum:

~Sc2 Life & Living processes 5a: Adaptation~

Homework Activity

Describe what the three different habitats in the table below would be like. These words and pictures will help you if you get stuck:

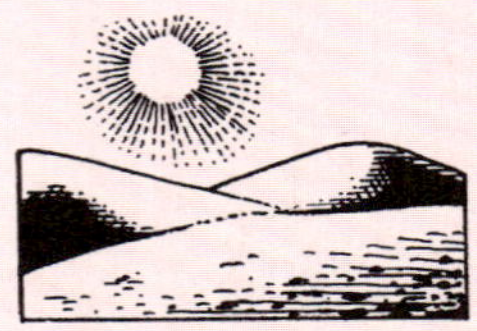

Very dry and hot

Gerbils, rattlesnakes, camels

Oak, ash and beech trees

Big tropical trees and bushes

Cactuses and tough spiky plants

Monkeys, large insects, parrots

Very hot with lots of rain

Squirrels, badgers and foxes

Not very hot or cold, some rain

	TROPICAL RAINFOREST	MIXED WOODLAND	HOT DESERT
Describe the weather			
What would the plants look like?			
What sort of animals would you find?			

IT'S BECOMING A HABITAT

~ Ask the family ~

Ask someone who knows about house plants to help you answer these questions. They may also be able to help you with the first part of the homework if you get stuck!

1 Find the names of some plants that people keep in dry, hot, sunny parts of the house. These come from desert regions.

2 Find some plants that like hot wet parts of the house, such as the bathroom. These plants come from rainforests.

3 Sketch the plants if you can.

4 Label your sketches with features that make them suited to their habitat, such as leaf size or shape. These are called 'adaptations'.

Background:

~A habitat is the place where a plant or animal lives.~

~Different habitats contain different kinds of plants and animals.~

~Many house plants come from different countries with different habitats. Some may come from deserts and others from tropical rainforests.~

~Plants from deserts often have fat leaves (succulents), or spiny leaves and fat stems (cactuses). They are often greyish or silvery. These plants store water.~

~Plants from a rainforest may have wide leaves that are often very dark or bright green. They may also have big, bright flowers, but desert plants can have bright flowers too.~

Aims:

~To understand the conditions that are necessary to keep a pet animal healthy and happy~

~To understand why pet owners should create natural conditions for their pets~

National Curriculum:

~Sc2 Life & Living processes 5b: Adaptation~

Background:

~Many pets were or still are wild animals.~

~They are suited to certain places and conditions (habitats). They are also suited to special activities.~

~Pets need a similar home to their wild habitat, and similar things to do.~

Homework Activity – Ask the family

Ask someone at home to help you with this activity.

1 Write an article for a magazine on how to care for a pet. Be sure to mention:

- What food it needs to stay in really good condition;
- How often it needs food and drink;
- What kind of place it lives and sleeps in;
- How often this pet, and the place where it lives, should be cleaned;
- What sort of exercise it needs;
- How often it needs to be seen by a vet;
- When it should breed.

2 Explain where you think your pet would have lived in the wild.

How is it adapted to the wild place it came from?

How can a person caring for it make its life as interesting as it would be in the wild?

How is a pet's life different from a wild animal's life?

WINTER SURVIVAL

Homework Activity

You may need to ask someone at home to help you or do some research using books or a CD ROM.

1 Find out how the animals named here survive the winter in Britain:

- Hedgehog
- Swallow
- Butterfly
- Grass snake
- Ptarmigan

2 Use what you find out to write an article for a children's wildlife magazine called Winter Survival. Draw some pictures to illustrate your article.

~ Ask the family ~

Ask someone at home or a neighbour who knows about plants and gardening to help you research these tasks

Plants have several special ways of surviving the winter. Try to find out how the four groups of plants below survive the winter:

For each group try to explain why it needs to use its special method of surviving until the spring.

a) Crocuses, onions and daffodils.

b) Oak, sycamore and ash trees.

c) Poppies, beans and tomatoes.

d) Fir trees, yew trees and pine trees.

Aim:

~To find out about the variety of ways in which plants and animals survive the winter~

National Curriculum:

~Sc2 Life & Living processes 2b: Adaptation~

Background:

~As you get closer to either the North or South Poles, winters last longer and longer.~

~Some animals and plants cannot survive the winter without changing the way they live.~

~Many plants and animals in Britain have special adaptations to help them survive the winter when it is cold and there is less sunlight. There is also less to eat in winter.~

LET US PREY

Aims:

~To understand the difference between prey and predator~

~To understand what adaptations a successful predator needs~

National Curriculum:

~Sc2 Life & Living processes 5c: Feeding relationships~

Background:

~A predator is an animal that hunts and eats another animal. It does not have to be big – it could be a spider or a centipede!~

~Prey animals are the animals that get eaten by the predator. They are often plant eaters, but some are predators too.~

Homework Activity

1 Make a list of the predators you might find in a wood or garden in this country.

2 What does each one eat?

3 What makes each one a really good predator?

4 Make a list or a labelled drawing to show what predators have in common.

~ Ask the family ~

1 Ask someone at home (or a neighbour) who knows about gardening to help you make a list of garden pests.

Garden pests are usually plant eaters. Many of them are the natural prey of garden predators.

2 Ask your family gardener to help you to name some of the garden predators.

3 Ask your family gardener which pests are eaten by each of the garden predators named.

HERE TODAY AND HERE TOMORROW

Homework Activity

To research these questions you will need to ask someone at home or use a textbook or CD ROM.

1 Find out why DDT was once used, especially in the 1950s and 60s.

2 Research the link between DDT and kestrels, sparrow hawks and owls.

3 Why have the numbers of some these birds almost returned to normal recently?

~ Ask the family ~

1 A chemical called Agent Orange was sprayed from helicopters during the Vietnam war by the USA to make all the leaves fall off the trees in the rain forest.

The US army did this so that they could see the people hiding in the rain forest. What other problems do you think were caused by the chemical in the rain forest food chain and for the local population?

2 One of the chemicals in Agent Orange is now found in pesticides used to kill slugs in gardens. Do you think this is a good way to handle garden pests?

3 Find out about some less harmful ways to prevent slugs from raiding the vegetable patch.

Aims:

~To be aware of chemicals used to kill plants and animals~

~To understand the wider environmental problems caused when these chemicals get into food chains~

~To understand that there are methods of control that cause less damage to the environment~

National Curriculum:

~Sc2 Life & Living processes 5e: Feeding relationships~

Background:

~Pesticides are chemicals used to kill pests or animals that eat our crops or garden plants.~

~A food chain is a sequence from plants through to predators.~

THE CATS HAVE DONE IT AGAIN

Aims:

~To understand what is meant by competition among animals~

~To understand that pet animals still behave in some ways as if they were wild~

National Curriculum:

~Sc2 Life & Living processes 5f: Competition~

Background:

~Wild animals compete with each other for food, a place to live, a mate, or a place to keep their young.~

~Some competition takes place between animals of the same species.~

~Some competition occurs between different species.~

Homework Activity

Research this activity using a CD ROM or a book from home or a library.

Every animal needs to eat, sleep, breed and hide sometimes.

Each animal needs to find enough food and safe places to live.

Sometimes, an animal wants to use the same food and shelter as another animal. This is called **competition.**

Find out why red squirrels are now very rare in Britain. Why has this happened?

~ Ask the family ~

Ask someone who has pet cats to help you to research these tasks.

1 How do pet cats mark where they live so that other cats stay away?

2 How do cats behave towards other cats coming into their garden? Describe how they drive other cats out.

3 When cats were wild animals, thousands of years ago, how would defending their territory help them to survive?

4 Find out if there are any other pet animals that mark and defend a territory. How do they do it?

WHAT'S THE MATTER?

Homework Activity

1 You are going to design a poster for younger children to explain the differences between solids, liquids and gases.

You will need a large piece of paper and lots of pictures of solids, liquids and gases from magazines. If you can't find enough pictures you could write the names of some things on your poster.

2 Put the pictures or words into the correct groups. Underneath each one, try to explain how you know it is a solid, liquid or gas.

~ Ask the family ~

With the help of someone at home try to find at least five solids, liquids or gases to complete the table below. Tick the properties that match your choice.
One example has been done to start you off.

PROPERTY	PLATE					
it has a fixed shape	✔					
it is runny						
it can be squashed						
it keeps its volume	✔					
it is not hard						
it is dense	✔					
it can be poured						
it is a …	solid					

Some things are difficult to put into a particular group. Did you find a difficult one? What was it?

Aim:

~To understand the differences between solids, liquids and gases in terms of their properties~

National Curriculum:

~Sc3 Materials and their Properties 1a: Solids, liquids and gases~

Background:

~Substances (matter) can be classified into three groups: solids, liquids and gases.~

~Substances are placed into these groups according to physical properties, such as whether they can be poured, squashed or stirred.~

Aims:

~To understand how the particles in solids, liquids and gases are arranged~

~To know that the particles within a substance are moving, and that the way they move depends upon whether the substance is a solid, a liquid or a gas~

National Curriculum:

~Sc3 Materials and their Properties 1b: Solids, liquids and gases~

Homework Activity

1 At school you will have learned about particles in a solid, a liquid and a gas. Imagine that the children at school are the particles in a substance. Which of the following situations do you think represents a solid, which is a liquid, and which is a gas?

In the playground where all the children are rushing around. Some children are bumping into each other and others are whizzing around on their own.

In the science lab where the children are doing some practical work. They are moving about slowly but, unfortunately, one or two children are bumping into each other.

In assembly where the children are sitting in rows, but they can't keep still. The Headteacher is talking and everyone else is fidgeting.

2 Draw three boxes, one for solid, one for liquid and one for gas. Inside each box show how the particles are arranged. Try to show the way they move.

~ Ask the family ~

1 Show the boxes you have drawn to someone at home and use them to explain what you know about particles in solids, liquids and gases.

2 Together, try to work out what will happen to the particles in a substance when ...

- **jelly sets**
- **water boils**
- **a saucepan gets hot**
- **butter melts**

3 Now plan and write a story about a particle for a children's magazine. In your story try to describe the particle's neighbours. Remember to mention how close the neighbours are and how much they move around. Give your story a funny title. Read it to someone at home when it is finished.

Background:

~Everything around us is made up of tiny particles. The way these particles are arranged and how they move depends on whether the substance is a solid, a liquid or a gas.~

~Particles in a solid are packed close together. They move to and fro quickly (vibrate) but never travel from place to place. Solids cannot change shape.~

~Particles in a liquid are more loosely packed. They can move about more freely than in a solid, although not as freely as in a gas. Liquids can change their shape but not their volume.~

~Particles in a gas move about freely. They can spread out to fill all the available space. Gases can change shape and volume.~

A QUESTION OF PARTICLES

Aims:

~To understand what is meant by 'particle theory'~

~To understand that particle theory accounts for the properties of solids, liquids and gases that we see every day~

National Curriculum:

~Sc3 Materials and their Properties 1c: Solids, liquids and gases~

Homework Activity

At school you will have done some work on 'particle theory'.

1 Use what you have learned to answer the 'True or False' questions below:

QUESTION	TRUE?	FALSE?
A gas can be squashed because the particles are far apart		
A liquid can be poured because the particles are spread out		
Fizzy drinks contain a gas		
A solid melts when the particles move more freely		
You can smell a perfume because the particles can spread out		
If a gas is heated all the particles slow down.		
When a solid cools the particles become smaller.		
When a gas spreads out we call this 'diffusion'		
If the answer is false then the question ends in a full-stop		

2 a) Find a fizzy drink in a bottle or can. Read the ingredients on the label. What gas do you think is put into fizzy drinks?

b) When you open a fizzy drink bottle or can, what happens to the gas? Can you explain what happens in terms of particles?

3 If someone walks into a room wearing perfume why can you smell it? Why do you think that you don't smell the perfume straight away? Hint: Think about gas particles bumping into each other. How does a perfume particle get to your nose?

A QUESTION OF PARTICLES

~ Ask the family ~

For the next question you need to find someone at home who knows about cars.

1 Why is it important to keep air out of the liquid (called 'brake fluid') that controls a car's brakes? Try to explain what happens when the brake pedal is pressed – use the idea of particles.

2 Bicycles have a cable to work the brakes. Explain what would happen between neighbouring particles if the cable broke?

3 Draw a poster to show how the differences between solids, liquids and gases can be explained using the idea of 'particles'.

Background:

~All substances are made up of particles.~

~The way the particles are arranged and how they move helps to explain the properties of solids, liquids and gases. This is known as 'particle theory'.~

~A solid keeps its shape because the particles are packed closely together.~

~A liquid takes up the shape of its container and can flow because the particles are free to move, but are loosely joined together.~

~A gas can spread out freely and take up any shape because the particles move about quickly in all directions and are not joined together.~

KNOW THE ELEMENTS

Aim:

~To revise the features of an element~

National Curriculum:

~Sc3 Materials and their Properties 1d: Elements~

Background:

~Solids, liquids and gases are made up of a small number of substances called elements.~

~Elements are themselves made up of tiny particles called atoms.~

~Elements are pure substances made up of only one type of atom.~

Homework Activity

Design a poster about elements to help someone revising for a test. Make sure that your poster includes the following information:

- What an element is.
- The two main groups that elements belong to.
- How many elements there are.
- The fact that elements are made up of tiny particles called atoms.

Find two more facts to add to this list.

Use a book or CD ROM to help you.

~ Ask the family ~

1 Show your poster to someone at home. Together, try to design a true/false quiz to help with revision. Test the quiz on your classmates or someone else at home.

2 Try to name at least five metals and five non-metals which are elements.

A CHEMICAL CODE

Homework Activity - Ask the family

You may need to use a textbook or a CD ROM to help you.

1 Symbols are often used to convey a message or to simplify information. Ask someone at home to help you to find out what the following symbols mean:

& $ % © ™ π

√ @ ♂ ♀

2 Find the symbols for the following elements:

- **magnesium** • **oxygen** • **iron** • **nickel** • **nitrogen**
- **chlorine** • **lead** • **gold** • **copper** • **carbon**

3 The symbols for road signs can be found in the Highway Code. Ask someone what the Highway Code is and why we should study it.

4 All the elements and their symbols can be found in the Periodic Table. How is this similar to the Highway Code? What information does it contain?

5 Fold a piece of plain A4 paper in half so that it opens like a greetings card. Use the paper to design a leaflet called 'The Chemical Code'. In your leaflet include:

- The reason why we use symbols;
- The symbols for some common elements;
- The reason why we put the elements in one table.

Aims:

~To understand why symbols are useful~

~To understand that elements can be represented by symbols~

~To know that all the elements and their symbols are present in the Periodic Table~

National Curriculum:

~Sc3 Materials and their Properties 1e: Elements~

Background:

~All chemicals are made of a small number of substances called elements.~

~Each element has its own symbol. The symbol for aluminium is Al, for example.~

~All the known elements are arranged in a chart called the Periodic Table.~

A CHANGE IN BEHAVIOUR

Aim:

~To understand that elements combine to form substances called compounds~

National Curriculum:

~Sc3 Materials and their Properties 1f: Compounds~

Background:

~Elements can be involved in chemical reactions to form new substances.~

~These new substances are called compounds.~

~Hydrogen and oxygen are elements which can combine to form the compound water.~

~Elements behave differently when they become part of a compound.~

Homework Activity

- Explain what the following words mean:

  a) element b) compound.

  Try to list five examples of each.
- Water is a compound. Describe some of the properties of water (how it behaves).
- Which elements make water?
- How do the elements in water differ from the compound?

~ Ask the family ~

1 Explain to someone at home the difference between an element and a compound.

2 Choose all the materials that are compounds from the list below:

- ammonia • oxygen • sodium chloride • copper sulphate • iron

3 The following materials are all compounds:

- **Rust**
- **Battery acid**
- **Carbon dioxide**
- **Table salt**
- **Methane (natural gas)**

Find out the elements that each compound is made of.

4 Elements and their compounds can be completely different. Find out how the elements in table salt behave when they are alone. How are these elements different from the compound called salt?

5 Prepare ten revision questions about elements and compounds. For each question write down the answers on a separate piece of paper.

ALL MIXED UP

Homework Activity

1 a) Look at the ingredients on the label of a fizzy drinks can. Draw the ingredients in a spider diagram.

b) Your drink is a mixture. Can you think of any other mixtures that you drink?

2 a) Your spider diagram contains different chemicals. Colour the elements blue and the compounds red.

b) Were the elements or compounds in the form of solids, liquids or gases before they went into your drink?

~ Ask the family ~

1 Show your spider diagram to someone at home. Use the diagram to explain why your drink is a mixture.

2 Together, try to think of at least five other mixtures. What substances do they contain? Are the substances elements or compounds?

3 Metal elements can be mixed to make alloys. The following 'metals' are alloys. Try to find out which metal elements each one contains:

- bronze
- brass
- steel
- stainless steel

Aim:

~ To understand that mixtures contain chemicals that are not combined together ~

National Curriculum:

~ Sc3 Materials and their Properties 1h: Mixtures ~

Background:

~ Chemicals that are not chemically combined are called mixtures. ~

~ Examples of mixtures include air, sea water, mineral water. ~

A USEFUL SEPARATION

Aim:

~To understand that it is sometimes useful to separate mixtures~

National Curriculum:

~Sc3 Materials and their Properties 1i: Mixtures~

Background:

~Chemicals that are not chemically combined are called mixtures.~

~It is sometimes useful to separate mixtures into their constituent parts.~

~Two mixtures that can usefully be separated are sea water and crude oil.~

Homework Activity

1 Write down what you understand by the word 'mixture'. Give five examples, including a liquid, a solid and a gas mixture.

2 Can you think of a reason why it could be useful to split a mixture up into the chemicals that it is made of.

3 Oil is a mixture of many chemicals. Find out how it is separated into different chemicals. Draw a diagram showing what oil is made of. Write down some uses for the three different parts of the oil mixture.

4 What is the correct term for the method of separating mixtures that you described for oil?

~ Ask the family ~

1 Show someone at home what you have done for the homework activity.

2 Look at the list of chemicals that oil is made of.

3 Discuss how our lives would be different without oil.

4 Write a story about the importance of separating one kind of mixture. Read your story to someone.

UNMIXING MIXTURES

Homework Activity

1 a) You will have separated some mixtures at school. Using your knowledge of separating mixtures, explain the following key words:
- **filtering**
- **evaporating**
- **distilling**
- **chromatography**

b) Describe one experiment you have done for each of the methods in (a).

2 a) Find out what is in the mixture we call 'rock salt'.

b) Plan an experiment to separate 'rock salt' into different chemicals.

~ Ask the family ~

1 Tell someone at home about the separation experiments you have done. Explain each method and why it is used.

2 Pick a method to separate each of the following mixtures:
- oil and water
- salty water
- sand and water
- muddy water
- orange clothes dye
- broken pottery in a sugar bowl

3 Imagine you are lost at sea with no fresh water. How can you get pure water from sea water?

4 How could you find out if the ink in a letter sent to the police is the same as that in an ink pen the police have found?

Aim:

~To revise some methods for separating mixtures~

National Curriculum:

~Sc3 Materials and their Properties 1i: Mixtures~

Background:

~Mixtures can be separated into useful chemicals.~

~Methods of separation include filtering, evaporating, distilling and chromatography.~

~The method chosen depends upon the properties of the mixture.~

HOT PROPERTY

Aims:

~To understand that most metals are shiny solids, and that heat and electricity can pass through them easily~

~To know that only a few metals are magnetic~

National Curriculum:

~Sc3 Materials and their Properties 1j: Metals and non-metals~

Background:

~Most metals have a shiny surface. This makes some metals attractive.~

~Heat passes easily through metals.~

~Metals are good thermal conductors. They are useful for making saucepans and radiators.~

~Metals are also good electrical conductors.~

Homework Activity

1 a) For thousands of years people have been using metal for jewellery, especially gold. Why do you think gold is popular for jewellery?

b) You may have some ornaments or decorations made of copper or brass at home. When they are clean, what do you notice about them?

c) Look at a saucepan. Which parts are metal and which are not? Why do you think this is?

2 a) Using a textbook or a CD ROM find out which metals are magnetic. (Hint: there are only three!)

b) When cans are recycled we need to separate the steel ones from the aluminium ones. How could we easily find out which is which?

~ Ask the family ~

Find out if anyone at home can carry out small electrical repairs, such as changing a plug. Ask if they would like to help you with the following questions.

1 Which parts of a plug does electricity travel through?

2 What are these parts made of?

3 Which parts of the plug are safe to touch?

4 What are these parts made of?

Homework Activity

1 Ask permission to cut some pictures out of a magazine or a newspaper.

Look for pictures of non-metals – any object that is not metal and contains no metal.

Cut the pictures out and make a collage.

Under each picture write down what makes that object useful, e.g. a pullover keeps you warm.

2 Using a textbook or a CD ROM try to find out the melting and boiling points of some non-metals. Compare them to those for metals. Is there a difference?

~ Ask the family ~

1 Go through the list of objects below with someone at home. Discuss why the objects are made out of particular materials.

- **electrical plug**
- **saucepan handle**
- **carpet**
- **hairdryer**
- **light switch**
- **mug**
- **table lamp**
- **oven gloves**

2 Design an experiment to find out whether a solid that you have been given is a non-metal. Think about the properties of metals and non-metals before you start. Read it to someone when it is finished.

Aims:

~To understand that non-metals can be solids, liquids or gases~

~To know that non-metals do not conduct heat or electricity easily~

National Curriculum:

~Sc3 Materials and their Properties 1k: Metals and non-metals~

Background:

~Substances which are not metal are called non-metals.~

~Non-metals can be solid, liquid or gas at normal temperatures. Most non-metals are either gases or solids which melt at low temperatures.~

~Most non-metals are very poor conductors of heat or electricity.~

A KEY PROPERTY

Aim:

~To use the properties of a substance to classify it as a metal or a non-metal~

National Curriculum:

~Sc3 Materials and their Properties 1l: Metals and non-metals~

Background:

~Substances can be defined as metals and non-metals.~

~Defining groups is called classifying.~

~A substance can be classified as a metal or non-metal on the basis of its properties, such as whether or not it is a good conductor of heat and electricity.~

Homework Activity - Ask the family

1 a) You are going to make a poster using different materials around the home. Make a collection of things that you can stick onto a poster with glue or sticky tape, e.g. kitchen foil, paper, a nail, a used match ...

b) Divide your objects into two groups: metals and non-metals. Now stick them onto your poster and label each group.

c) Find out what each object is used for. What is special about each object that makes it useful?

2 a) Find out exactly what each of the items in your poster is made of.

b) Add the uses and materials to your poster.

c) Look carefully at your finished poster to see if you can find any big differences between the labels on metals and non-metals.

GETTING PHYSICAL

Homework Activity

1 a) What is the difference between a solid, a liquid and a gas?

b) What changes take place when ice melts? Does a new chemical form?

c) If you boiled some water, how could you turn the steam back into ice?

2 a) The changes that take place in 1(b) and 1(c) are called physical changes. How are they different from what happens when iron changes to rust?

b) If sugar is dissolved in tea, how could you get the sugar back again? Is this a physical or chemical change?

~ Ask the family ~

1 Explain to someone at home what a 'physical change' is.

2 Go through the following situations together and work out which ones involve a physical change:

- **butter melting**
- **water boiling**
- **a candle burning**
- **ice melting**
- **a window 'steaming up'**
- **sugar dissolving in tea**
- **a car rusting**
- **a pear ripening**

3 In each of the physical changes you found, what is the name given to the temperature when they occurred?

Aims:

~To understand what a physical change means~

~To recognise that different materials change state at different temperatures~

National Curriculum:

~Sc3 Materials and their Properties 2a,c: Physical changes~

Background:

~The properties of a substance can change without altering the substance. When this happens, we say there has been a 'change of state' or a 'physical change'.~

~After a physical change, the new substance can easily be turned back into the original one, e.g. water can easily be turned back into ice.~

THE RIGHT SOLUTION

Aims:

~To understand that some substances dissolve in liquids~

~To discover that increasing the temperature of the liquid helps a solute to dissolve more quickly~

National Curriculum:

~Sc3 Materials and their Properties 2b: Physical changes~

Background:

~Solid substances that dissolve are known as 'solutes'.~

~Solutes may dissolve in different liquids (known as 'solvents') and at different temperatures.~

~The solubility of a solute increases as the solvent's temperature rises.~

Homework Activity

1 a) What happens when you put sugar into water? Use the key words below in your explanation:
- **dissolve**
- **solute**
- **solvent**
- **solution**

b) Does it make a difference if you put sugar into hot water? Try to use the key word 'solubility' in your answer.

2 Plan an investigation to find out how the temperature of water affects the solubility of sugar. Your plan should contain:

- a prediction – using anything you know about particles;
- the key words from question 1;
- a list of the equipment you will need;
- a description of how you will use your equipment;
- details about how you will make your test fair.

~ Ask the family ~

1 Explain to someone at home what is meant by the words **solvent, solute** and **solution.**

2 Different solvents are used to make paints and varnishes, including nail varnish. The same solvents are needed to remove spilt paint and varnish. See if you can find any cleaning solvents at home. What are their names?

3 When you take clothes to be dry-cleaned, why is it helpful to tell the cleaners when something unusual has been spilt on them?

AN EXPANDING PROBLEM

Homework Activity

At school you will have seen or done some experiments that involve expansion or contraction.

Design a poster to show some of these experiments. In your poster, try to explain what causes expansion and contraction.

~ Ask the family ~

1 Show your poster to someone at home. Use it to explain to them what 'expansion' and 'contraction' mean.

2 Explain how expansion or contraction is involved in the following situations:

- When a metal bridge is built, small gaps are left at the ends of the bridge.
- When the air in a hot-air balloon is heated the balloon rises.
- The water tank in an empty house is emptied before the winter.
- Small gaps are left between the metal parts of a railway track.
- Mercury can be used to make a thermometer to measure temperature
- The wires between telegraph poles are more slack in the summer.

Aim:

~To understand that materials expand and contract and that the forces involved are sometimes very large~

National Curriculum:

~Sc3 Materials and their Properties 2e: Physical changes~

Background:

~When a solid such as a metal is heated it becomes larger. This is known as expansion.~

~If the solid is then cooled it will shrink. This is known as contraction.~

~As expansion or contraction takes place a force is produced and this can sometimes be considerable.~

WATER RULES, OK

Aims:

~To understand the importance of water on Earth and how it affects every part of life~

~To know that water expands when it freezes~

National Curriculum:

~Sc3 Materials and their Properties 2b: Physical changes~

Background:

~Water is the most important solvent on Earth.~

~All living things use water as a solvent.~

~Many rocks are formed or changed by the action of water.~

~Water expands when it freezes.~

Homework Activity

Water is one of the most important liquids on Earth.

1 Look at each of the words or phrases below and try to imagine a world without water:

- **weather**
- **flowers**
- **breakfast**
- **fish and chips**
- **holidays**
- **brushing your teeth**
- **snowballs**
- **feeling sad**
- **seeds**

2 Now make a poster to show how important water is.

~ Ask the family ~

You have learned that substances contract when they become colder. Ask as many people as you can what happens to watery things when they freeze.

What happens to soup when it is put into the freezer?

What can happen to milk when it is left on the doorstep in winter?

What does a driver need to add to the water in a car every winter?

What can happen to water pipes in winter?

Now write down what happens to water when it gets cold enough to freeze. Does it expand or contract?

Homework Activity - Ask the family

This task may take a day or so to complete.

HAZARD WARNING!
Never place glass or metal in the freezer, use only plastic. Ask someone to help you with this task.

1 Find a small (empty) plastic bottle used for fizzy drinks. Fill the bottle with water and screw the lid on tightly. Place the bottle in a plastic bag and tie it up. Now place the bottle in your freezer for a day.

(Hint: If you can't find a plastic bottle, use an empty paper milk carton instead.)

2 What happened to the water when you put it into the freezer? What did the bottle do? Write a report of what happened and include the word 'expand'.

3 When water gets into cracks in a rock, what do you think could happen to the rock if the water turned to ice? How would this help the process of weathering?

4 Falling rocks can be dangerous, especially for climbers.

Draw a safety poster warning climbers of the dangers of falling rocks. In your poster explain how rocks can crack and fall off suddenly.

5 The Romans used to light fires under rocks until they were very hot, and then throw cold water onto them. What were they trying to do to the rocks?

Aims:

~To understand that rocks can be weathered by expanding and contracting~

~To know that the freeezing of water in cracks in rocks can also cause weathering~

National Curriculum:

~Sc3 Materials and their Properties 2f: Geological changes~

Background:

~When rocks heat up in the sun they get bigger (expand). When they cool down at night they shrink (contract).~

~Repeated expansion and contraction of rock causes it to crack. This is known as weathering.~

~If water gets into cracks in a rock, it may freeze at night. Water expands when it turns to ice and this can enlarge cracks until pieces of rock break away and fall off.~

ROCK AROUND THE CLOCK

Aims:

~To understand that the materials that make rocks can be used again and again~

~To know that this process is called the rock cycle~

National Curriculum:

~Sc3 Materials and their Properties 2g: Geological changes~

Homework Activity

People who study rocks are called geologists. They study rocks because they want to find out how the Earth was formed and how it has changed. To do this they need to understand the Rock Cycle. Test yourself to see if you would make a good geologist.

1 Your teacher may give you a copy of the rock cycle like the one below. Match the words in the box with the descriptions in the rock cycle.

These rocks form very slowly. They are made when other rocks get hot or are put under pressure.

These rocks are made when hot liquid rock cools. Sometimes this can happen quickly, such as in a volcano.

Rocks in the open air become weak and may crack.

These rocks form when rock or mud is squashed. They may contain fossils.

A weak rock is easily worn away by rain or rivers or wind.

Mud and small pieces of rock are dropped by rivers and streams when the water moves slowly.

Small pieces of rock are carried away by rivers or streams.

sedimentary	transport	metamorphic	erosion
deposition	igneous	weathering	

ROCK AROUND THE CLOCK

~ Ask the family ~

Use the picture of a volcano below to explain to someone at home how the rock cycle works.

Copy the picture onto a large piece of plain paper so that you can make a big poster of the rock cycle. Use the words from the homework activity to show where each part of the rock cycle fits. Colour your poster to make it look attractive.

Background:

~The minerals that make up a rock are used again and again. This process is called the rock cycle. It shows what might happen to a rock in the future and what may have happened to the rock in the past.~

~The rock cycle includes three main types of rock: sedimentary, metamorphic and igneous. The processes that form these rocks may occur quickly or very slowly. Altogether, the rock cycle may take millions of years to complete.~

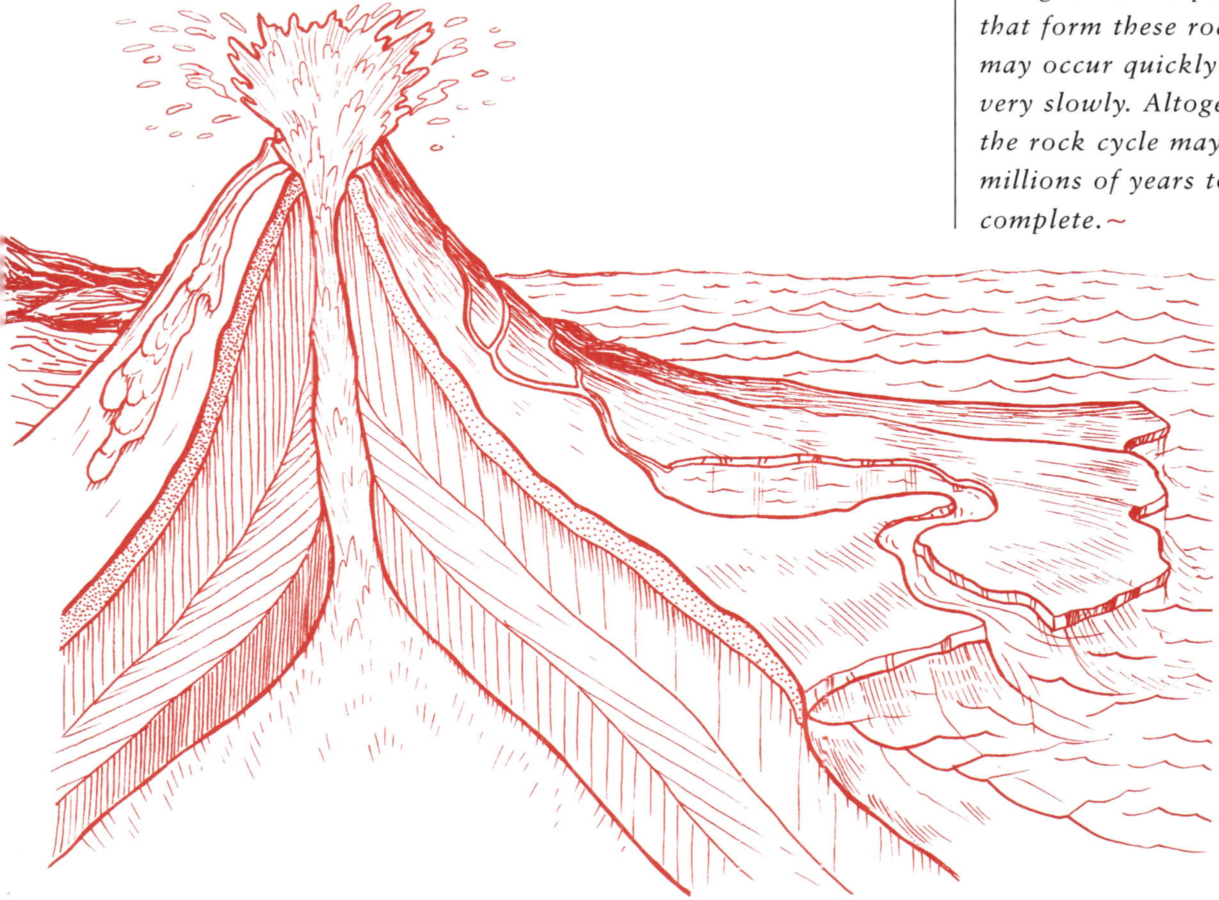

WHAT GROUP IS THAT?

Aims:

~To know that rocks can be put into three main groups and that grouping things is called classification~

~To be able to use a key to sort rocks into groups~

National Curriculum:

~Sc3 Materials and their Properties 2h: Geological changes~

Homework Activity

1 We can sort rocks into groups by using a key like the one below. Arranging things we find into groups is called classifying.

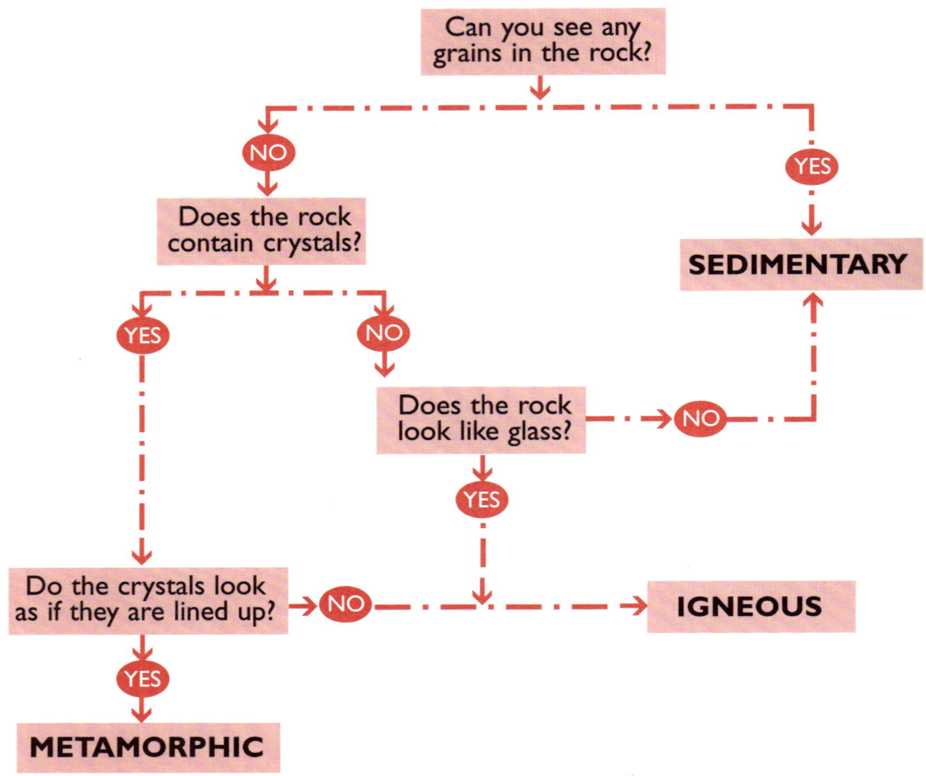

WHAT GROUP IS THAT?

2 The descriptions below belong to some rocks that a geologist has found. Use the key opposite to help her to classify the rocks.

Rock 1: This rock contains lots of grains like sand. I can scratch it with a knife, so it is not very hard.

Rock 2: I found this rock near an old volcano – it is black and looks like glass. It is very hard!

Rock 3: This rock is fairly hard. It is grey and has tiny crystals in it. The crystals are arranged neatly.

Rock 4: This is a hard rock with many big pink and white crystals in it. The crystals are very untidy.

~ Ask the family ~

1 Go outside with someone at home and have a look at all the different types of rock that you can find. You do not have to be in the countryside. Look at the kerbstones outside your house, or the fronts of buildings or pieces of sculpture. Remember that bricks are not natural rocks.

2 Make a table describing the rocks you find.

3 Can you use your key to identify the rocks you found?

Background:

~Rocks can be put into three main groups. These big groups are called sedimentary, igneous and metamorphic.~

~Arranging things in groups is called 'classifying'.~

*~We can use a **key** to help us to classify objects. A key asks a series of questions about the object to help you to decide which group it belongs in.~*

~Before we can classify a rock we must be able to describe it.~

DOES ANYTHING STAY THE SAME?

Aims:

~To know that most substances are the result of chemical reactions~

~To understand that there are different types of reactions~

~To know that chemical reactions can either be useful or an inconvenience~

National Curriculum:

~Sc3 Materials and their Properties 2j,l,m,n: Chemical reactions~

Background:

~Practically everything, including living things, is made by chemical reactions.~

~Chemical reactions are taking place all the time. For example, iron oxidises to make rust and dead plants oxidise in a compost heap.~

Homework Activity

Almost everything around us is the result of a chemical reaction.

1 a) Name at least five things that are made by a chemical reaction.

b) At school you will have learnt about different types of chemical reaction. Explain what happens in each of the following chemical reactions:

- **oxidation**
- **decomposition**

2 Name some ways of slowing down the reactions in question 1(a).

~ Ask the family ~

1 Explain to someone at home what the words 'oxidise' and 'decompose' mean.

2 Together, try to decide which of the following situations involve oxidation and which involve decomposition:

- Suzanna burns her toast at breakfast time
- Samier's car is going rusty
- Rob lights a candle
- Barbara polishes her brass ornaments every week
- Hoi-Yan brews some beer
- Lee eats a bag of crisps
- A cell dies

3 Divide the list above into reactions which are useful to us and those which are an inconvenience.

ENERGISE!

Homework Activity

1 a) Write down everything that you have eaten today.

b) What did all the different foods you ate today give you?

c) Which foods gave you the most energy?

2 a) When food provides energy in your body a chemical reaction called 'respiration' is taking place. We can write respiration as a word equation. What is the word equation for respiration?

b) Can you think of another chemical reaction that gives out energy?

c) What name do we give to reactions that give out energy?

~ Ask the family ~

1 Explain the connection between chemical reactions and energy to someone at home.

2 Discuss how the following things are involved in chemical reactions that give out energy:

petrol sugar compost coal

3 For each reaction in question 2, write down how the energy that is released could be used.

4 Alcohol is made by a process that gives out energy. What is this process called?

Aims:

~To understand that chemical reactions can produce energy~

~To begin to see chemical reactions as word equations~

National Curriculum:

~Sc3 Materials and their Properties 2k,o: Chemical reactions~

Background:

~Energy may be released when a chemical reaction takes place.~

~Energy is released when a fuel, like coal or gas, is burned. The release of energy can sometimes be useful.~

A CHANGE FOR THE BETTER

Aim:

~To understand that useful products can be made from chemical reactions~

National Curriculum:

~Sc3 Materials and their Properties 2m: Chemical reactions~

Background:

~When chemicals react together to make a new substance we call this a 'chemical change' or a 'chemical reaction'.~

~Some chemical changes can be useful to us.~

Homework Activity

1 You will need a sheet of A4 plain paper folded in half for this project. The project is to write a revision leaflet called 'chemical reactions' for someone in your class. Include the following points:

- An explanation of what a chemical reaction is;
- Some examples of reactions you have done yourself;
- Some examples of reactions that your teacher has shown you;
- Some examples of useful products that you can make in a reaction.

Show that reactions are not always useful.

2 Design a quiz to go at the end of your leaflet (and write the answers on a separate sheet).

~ Ask the family ~

1 Show your revision leaflet to someone at home. Can they answer the questions? Be there to help them if they get stuck.

2 Discuss some of the materials (substances) that things in your house are made of. Write down the name of the material and what the article is used for. Design a table to summarise what you have discovered.

3 Now use your table to design a poster showing useful materials and what they are from.

FOR BETTER OR FOR WORSE

Homework Activity

Design a 'True or False' quiz about chemical reactions. You must know what the answers are yourself. Be sure to include the following points (you may need to look them up before you begin):

- Whether a chemical change makes a compound;
- What happens to the weight of the chemicals in a chemical change;
- How a chemical change is different from a physical change;
- Whether you can turn the product back into the things you started with.

Invent some true/false examples of chemical changes.

~ Ask the family ~

1 After you complete the task above, show your quiz to someone at home. If they get any answers wrong, tell them the correct answer and explain the question again.

2 Discuss at least five chemical reactions that take place in one of the following places:
a) the kitchen; or b) a car

Write down whether the chemical changes you chose are useful or not.

Aims:

~To understand that chemical reactions take place in many materials~

~To know that chemical changes can either be useful or an inconvenience~

National Curriculum:

~Sc3 Materials and their Properties 2m,n: Chemical reactions~

Background:

~When chemicals react together to make a new substance we call this a 'chemical change' or a 'chemical reaction'.~

~Most materials are involved in some kind of chemical change.~

~Chemical changes can be either useful or an inconvenience to us.~

GLOBAL WARNING?

Aim:

~To understand the possible effects on the environment of burning fossil fuels~

National Curriculum:

~Sc3 Materials and their Properties 2p: Chemical reactions~

Background:

~Fossil fuels (coal, oil and gas) are used in power stations to generate electricity.~

~Although the process is relatively cheap, many people are worried that burning fossil fuels is making the world warmer. This is called global warming.~

~Burning coal to heat homes causes air pollution, particularly in towns and cities.~

Homework Activity

1 a) What is a fossil fuel?

b) Why are many people worried about the burning of fossil fuels?

2 a) Find out what global warming means. How does burning fossil fuels contribute to global warming?

b) Name three problems caused by global warming.

c) Fossil fuels are often used to make electricity. Are there other ways of making electricity?

~ Ask the family ~

1 Electricity companies say that "turning your thermostat down by 1°C helps to reduce your bills by up to 10%". Ask someone to explain what this means. How does this help us reduce global warming?

2 Find out how your grandparents used to heat their homes.

3 Ask an older member of your family if they used coal to keep their homes warm. Were there any special problems with coal fires that we do not have with central heating?

In 1952, 4,000 people died in London because of coal-burning fires. The combination of smoke and fog made a lethal mixture of poisonous gases called 'smog'. People died as a result of inhaling the smog. Now, only 'smokeless' fuel is allowed to be burned in cities.

4 Imagine you are a news reporter working in London in 1952. Describe the effects of the smog and why it has happened.

ANY OLD IRON?

Homework Activity

1 Why don't most metals stay shiny and hard forever?

2 The process that you described in question 1 is called 'corrosion'. What kind of metals corrode by 'rusting'?

3 Look at the picture below. Which of the nails will rust? Explain why.

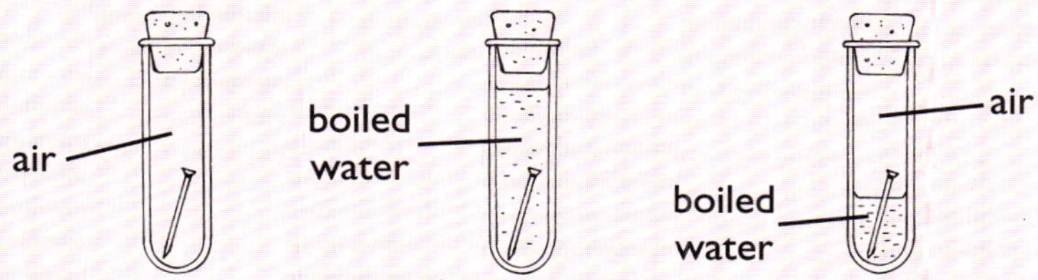

~ Ask the family ~

There are many things in and around every home that can corrode or rust. Ask someone at home to help you with the following questions:

1 Drainpipes are now often made of plastic, but they used to be made out of iron. What did the rain do to the iron drain pipes?

2 Gates and bridges are also made of iron. How can they be protected from air and water so that they do not rust?

3 There are objects inside the home that react with the air. Ask someone at home what happens to the following things when they are not properly cared for:
- **brass ornaments**
- **copper pipes**
- **saucepans**

4 Design a leaflet for a DIY store. In it, explain how to protect different metals from corrosion. You may be able to find some information in stores to help you with your design.

Aim:

~To understand that metals can react with oxygen, water and acid~

National Curriculum:

~Sc3 Materials and their Properties 3a: Metals; 2n: Chemical reactions~

Background:

~Metals can be attacked by water, air or other substances. This process is called 'corrosion'.~

~Rust is the result of corrosion of iron and steel. Corrosion of iron and steel is therefore called rusting.~

REACTIVITY LEAGUE

Aims:

~*To know that displacement reactions take place between metals and their compounds*~

~*To know that the reactivity series can be used to make predictions about the reactions between metals*~

National Curriculum:

~*Sc3 Materials and their Properties 3b,d: Metals*~

Homework Activity - Ask the family

1 Explain to someone at home what the following words or phrases mean. Use examples to help them to understand.

- **reactivity series**
- **competition**
- **displacement reaction**

2 Work with someone at home to predict who will win the 'games' opposite. Remember that the winner will always be the most reactive metal in the game.

3 Guess what the 'goal difference' will be. Remember that the further apart the metals are in the reactivity series, the bigger the goal difference is. (*The first game is already done for you.*)

REACTIVITY LEAGUE

HOME TEAM	SCORE	SCORE	AWAY TEAM
Potassium **Oxide** Dolphins	**1**	**0**	Sodium Spartans
Magnesium Magpies			Copper **Oxide** Raptors
Iron Lions			Calcium **Oxide** Cougars
Sodium Spartans			Magnesium **Oxide** Magpies
Tin **Oxide** Blue Jays			Iron Lions
Copper **Oxide** Raptors			Potassium Dolphins
Calcium Cougars			Tin **Oxide** Blue Jays

4 One of the teams in each game already has the 'oxide' trophy. Using your results from question one, say which team keeps, loses or wins the 'oxide' trophy.

5 The team that wins the 'oxide' trophy can then use it in its name, e.g. Sodium Oxide Spartans. You can write down the final results in the following way:

Sodium Spartans + Magnesium Oxide Magpies

→ Sodium Oxide Spartans + Magnesium Magpies

Now write down the results of the other games in the same way. After that, fill in the match results on the chart.

Background:

~Metals can be put into a league table based upon how reactive they are. This league table is called the Reactivity Series of Metals.~

~We can work out the order of the Reactivity Series by setting up competitions between metals, such as a competition to possess oxygen.~

~When a metal 'wins' oxygen from another metal we say it has displaced the oxygen. This is what is meant by a displacement reaction.~

THE HISTORY OF HEAVY METAL

Aims:

~To understand that metals can be placed into a league table based upon their reactivity~

~To know that this league table is known as the Reactivity Series~

National Curriculum:

~Sc3 Materials and their Properties 3c: Metals~

Homework Activity

Begin by explaining to someone what the Reactivity Series of Metals shows. Tell them about some of the work that you have been doing in science. Ask them if they would like to help you with the following questions.

1. Look at the time line below. It shows roughly when certain metals were first used.
2. What do you notice about the order in which metals were discovered and Reactivity Series? What are the similarities and differences between the two?
3. Gold is an unreactive metal. Why do we not make cars and bridges from gold?
4. Gold is the most unreactive metal. Why do you think it might not have been discovered first.

COPPER	GOLD	LEAD	SILVER
7,000 BC	5,000 BC	3,500 BC	2,400 BC

THE HISTORY OF HEAVY METAL

5 What happens to copper when it is left out in the open? (Hint: the roofs of some old buildings, such as churches, are made of copper. What colour are they?)

6 Aluminium is a reactive metal. Why do we use it to make saucepans, cans and aeroplane bodies? Why doesn't it corrode away? (Tricky! You may have to do some research from a book or a CD ROM.)

~ Ask the family ~

Ask someone at home to help you carry out a mini-project about metals. In your project you must explain:

- When each metal was first used;
- What the metals were used for;
- How reactive each metals is;
- What each metal is used for today.

You can add more topics to this list if you wish.

Background:

~Metals often react with things around them, e.g. iron reacts with oxygen and water to form rust.~

~Because some metals are more reactive than others, they can be arranged in a league table called the Reactivity Series – the most reactive at the top, and the least reactive at the bottom.~

~Metals were discovered in an order very similar to the Reactivity Series. This is because more reactive metals are found as compounds, not as pure elements in rocks.~

YOU'VE GOT *pH*ABULOUS SKIN!

Aim:

~To understand that 'pH' is a measure of how acidic or alkaline a solution is~

National Curriculum:

~Sc3 Materials and their Properties 3e: Acids and bases~

Homework Activity

1 a) In your science book write down what the following words mean:

- **acid**
- **alkali**
- **neutral**

b) Draw the pH scale and label it with 'acid', 'alkali' and 'neutral'.

2 Below is a list of substances you might find at home. They are either acid or alkali.

- **orange juice**
- **indigestion tablets**
- **vinegar**
- **baking soda**

Plan an investigation to find out whether they are acid or alkali. Remember the rules for a fair test.

~ Ask the family ~

1. Ask some people at home whether they use any special soaps, face creams or baby oil. Have a look at the packets or bottles that they come in.
2. Does the label tell you what the pH of the product is?
3. Ask the person who uses the product why they use it. Why should we use a product with a pH of 5.5 for our skin?
4. Normal soap has a pH of about 10. What do you think this might do to your skin?
5. Find out how soap is made. You will need to research this for yourself in books. Now can you suggest why soap has such a high pH?

Background:

~ When a substance is dissolved in water the solution may be acidic, alkaline or neutral. ~

~ The strength of an acid or an alkali is measured in pH units. ~

~ The pH scale runs from 1 through to 14. ~

~ If the pH number is from 1 to 6 it is an acid. ~

~ If the pH number is from 8 to 14 it is an alkali. ~

~ pH 7 is neutral. ~

~ Strong acids have a pH number close to 1. ~

~ Strong alkalis have a pH number close to 14. ~

~ A pH near to 7 is not a strong acid or alkali. ~

USEpHUL PAPER!

Aim:

~To understand that some substances change colour when they react with acids, alkalis or neutral solutions and that these substances are called indicators~

National Curriculum:

~Sc3 Materials and their Properties 3f: Acids and bases~

Homework Activity

Jenny was asked by her science teacher to see if she could find acids and alkalis at home. She was given some indicator paper to help her. Jenny wrote her results in a table but she didn't finish it. Can you help her to complete the table?

1 First, you will need to find a copy of the pH scale from your school classbook.

SUBSTANCE IN THE HOUSE	COLOUR OF INDICATOR PAPER	ACID	ALKALI	NEUTRAL
milk	yellow			
vinegar	orange			
lemonade	orange			
shampoo	green			
oven cleaner	violet			
soap	blue			
baby oil	yellow-orange			
toothpaste	blue-green			
washing soda	indigo			
mineral water	green			

2 Complete Jenny's table by ticking the correct box to say which substance you think is an acid, which is an alkali, and which is neutral.

3 Try to find out what pH number each substance has. What is the best way to do this?

USEpHUL PAPER!

~ Ask the family ~

1 Explain to someone at home what indicators are used for.

2 Discuss together why the following people need to use indicators: *(You may need to do some research from a book or a CD ROM.)*

Mr Johnson is a wheat farmer. What will he test the pH of, and what help will this give him?

Mrs Begum is a keen gardener. How can pH help her to find out which plants will grow best in her garden?

Ms Porter is a chemist who makes toothpaste. What must she do to make sure that the toothpaste she makes helps everyone's teeth stay healthy?

Mr Stone is concerned about air pollution. Every time it rains he collects a sample. What does he do with the rain water to find out if it is polluting? Why does he test the rain water rather than the air?

3 Mr Stone is not a scientist. Ask someone to help you to plan an investigation to help him find out if local air pollution is getting worse.

Background:

~ Substances which change colour when they react with acids, alkalis or neutral solutions are called indicators.~

~Some indicators are one colour for acid and another colour for alkali.~

~Some indicators have more than one colour depending on the strength of the acid or alkali.~

~A common indicator used at school is 'pH paper' or 'universal indicator'.~

A STINGING SOLUTION

Aims:

~To understand that acids and alkalis can be neutralised~

~To know that neutralisation has useful everyday applications~

National Curriculum:

~Sc3 Materials and their Properties 3h: Acids and bases~

Background:

~If an acid and an alkali of equal strength are mixed together the final solution will be neutral.~

~A neutral substance has a pH number of 7 and is neither an acid nor an alkali.~

~The process of making an acid or alkali neutral is called neutralisation.~

~Neutralisation has many everyday uses. Indigestion tablets help to neutralise stomach acid, for example.~

Homework Activity

1 If you add an acid to an alkali you can make a neutral substance.

a) What does the word neutral mean?

b) Imagine that you are a scientist. You have been asked to find out why the fish in a farmer's lake seem to be dying. After testing the lake you find out that the water has a pH of 4.

Is the lake water an acid or alkali?

c) How could you make the lake neutral?

2 Part of the pain of bee and wasp stings is due to acid or alkali. A bee sting is acidic with a pH of 6, whilst a wasp sting is alkali with a pH of 8.

a) What can you add to the sting if you are stung by:

- **a bee?**
- **a wasp?**

b) What common substances around the home could you use to neutralise a sting?

~ Ask the family ~

1 Ask someone at home what 'indigestion' is. Have they suffered from it themselves?

2 Why do people get indigestion?

3 Find out what happens in your stomach when you get indigestion. (You may need to look in a textbook or use a CD ROM.)

4 People suffering from indigestion sometimes take an 'indigestion tablet'. What do you think is in one of these tablets – an acid or an alkali?

ACID DROPS

Homework Activity

In Northern Europe, acid rain has destroyed thousands of trees and poisoned lakes full of fish. Answer the following questions about acid rain. (You might need to do some research from a book or a CD ROM.)

1 a) Find out what causes acid rain.
   b) Find out what pH acid rain might have?
   c) What effect will acid rain have on soil?
   d) What other damage might acid rain cause?
   e) Draw a picture showing the damage that acid rain causes.

2 Why do you think that Northern Europe might be affected more than other parts of Europe?

~ Ask the family ~

Ask an older member of your family to help you with the following questions:

1 Are there any stone statues near where you live? Have they changed in any way since they were erected?

2 Go and look at old buildings nearby, or a cemetery. Do they show any signs of their age? What are the signs of age that you can see?

3 Old iron bridges often show signs of age too. What do you think these signs might be?

4 Why have buildings, bridges and gravestones aged more quickly in recent years?

Aim:

~To understand that acids in the atmosphere attack rock and metal and affect the growth of plants and animals~

National Curriculum:

~Sc3 Materials and their Properties 3i: Acids and bases~

Background:

~Due to air pollution by industrialised countries, rain water has become more acidic.~

~The effect on nature has been disastrous, particularly in parts of Northern Europe.~

~Acid rain also affects stone and metal structures.~

STICK 'EM UP

Aims:

~To know that insulators can be given an electric charge when they are rubbed and that this is called static electricity~

~To understand that charged objects attract or repel each other~

~To know that static electricity can sometimes be dangerous~

National Curriculum:

~Sc4 Physical Processes 1a, b: Static charge~

Background:

~Some materials, such as plastic or rubber, do not allow electricity to pass through them. They are called 'insulators'. Rubbing an insulator with a cloth can give it an electric charge.~

Homework Activity

For this project you will need a small plate, some cling film, a cloth and a scrap of tissue paper or newspaper. Ask permission before you begin.

1 Tear your paper into pieces about the size of the nail on your little finger. Drop them onto your plate as you work, and then stretch the cling film over the top. Do not allow the cling film to touch the paper. Make sure it is nice and tight.

2 Rub the cling film with the cloth – take care not to press too hard. What happens to the paper?

3 Touch the cling film with your finger near to one of the pieces of paper. What happens? Why do you think this happens?

~ Ask the family ~

1 Show your 'trick' to someone at home and try to explain why it happens.

2 Ask them if they know a trick using static electricity. If they do, ask them to show it to you and try to puzzle out how it works.

3 Ask someone what the word 'static' means. Discuss with them why it is called this.

4 Static electricity can be very useful. It is used in printing and photocopying, and even for spraying special paints. But static electricity can also be dangerous. Together, think of some places where an electric spark might be dangerous.

5 Research and write an article for a school science magazine about static electricity. You could call it 'Static Magic'. Read your article to someone at home.

Background:

~ The charge on an insulator cannot move because an insulator does not allow electricity to flow. The fact that the electric charge cannot move gives it the name of 'static electricity'. ~

~ Two objects carrying the same electric charge will move apart (repel one another). If their charges are opposite, they will move together (attract one another). ~

~ A material which does conduct electricity (a conductor) will allow the charge to flow away from a charged insulator it touches. ~

~ An insulator may build up enough charge to make a spark jump to a conductor. This can be very dangerous when there is petrol present, such as when aircraft or vehicles take on fuel. ~

OH NO, THEY'VE GONE OFF AGAIN!

Aims:

~To research a problem caused by traditional Christmas tree light circuits and explain why it happens~

~To apply knowledge and understanding of circuits to design an improved Christmas tree light circuit~

~To research the layout of home electrical circuits with the help of an adult~

National Curriculum:

~Sc4 Physical processes 1c,d: Current in circuits~

Background:

~At school you will have learned about two different types of electrical circuit.

The circuits you learn about at school also exist in your home.~

Homework Activity

Ask if you can look at some Christmas tree lights!

Hazard warning: You will have to ask an adult to help or supervise you if you plug them in!

1 a) What is it about Christmas tree lights that drives everyone crazy?

b) What do the manufacturers do to try to solve this problem? Look carefully at each of the bulbs.

2 Draw a circuit diagram for a new improved version of Christmas tree lights that solves the problem.

~ Ask the family ~

Ask someone at home to help to you research these tasks. DIY books may also contain information that will help you.

1 Draw a circuit diagram for staircase lights that can be turned off and on from the top and bottom of the stairs.

2 Find someone who can explain what a ring main is in a house. (This may be very difficult. Don't worry if you can't work it out.)

DESIGNER CIRCUITS

~ Ask the family ~

Ask someone at home to help you with these tasks. Choose someone with time to spare who enjoys learning new things.

1 Teach someone at home the symbols for common parts to electrical circuits.

2 Work together to draw some circuit diagrams, using as many symbols as possible. Try the circuits below.

Homework Activity

Imagine you are a designer for a company that makes electrical circuits for homes and small businesses.

For each of the three customers below, draw a circuit diagram and explain how it works in short and simple sentences. Don't confuse them with scientific words.

Mrs. Shah: *I want a doorbell that works from either the front or back door, but grandma lives with us and she is deaf. Can you design a circuit that can help us?*

Mr. Green: *Our receptionist works at a desk just inside the entrance to our company premises. The street is right outside, and we worry about intruders coming in. Can you design a circuit that will tell people in the office when someone comes in or out so we can check that the receptionist is safe?*

Ms. Watson: *I run a small engineering company. My employees keep getting electric shocks from the big powerful machines. Can you design a safe way to turn the machines on and off?*

Aims:

~To design some circuits to solve customers, problems as if you were working for an electrical company~

~To learn how to use electrical symbols to draw circuit diagrams~

National Curriculum:

~Sc4 Physical processes 1d,e: Currents in circuits~

Background:

~In this activity you will be using what you have learned at school to design simple circuits with switches, wires, bulbs, buzzers, motors, electromagnets or relays. Don't worry if you do not know what all of these parts are.~

ON YOUR BIKE!

Aims:

~To research the uses and problems of friction~

~To research the most suitable lubricant for a number of different situations~

National Curriculum:

~Sc4 Physical processes 1e: Forces and linear motion~

Background:

~Friction is a force that resists movement when two things rub together.~

~Friction can help one surface to grip another, such as the soles of shoes on slippery ground.~

~Friction is a problem for many machines with moving parts.~

~Lubricants are used to reduce friction in motors and machines.~

Homework Activity

1 Study this drawing of a bicycle.

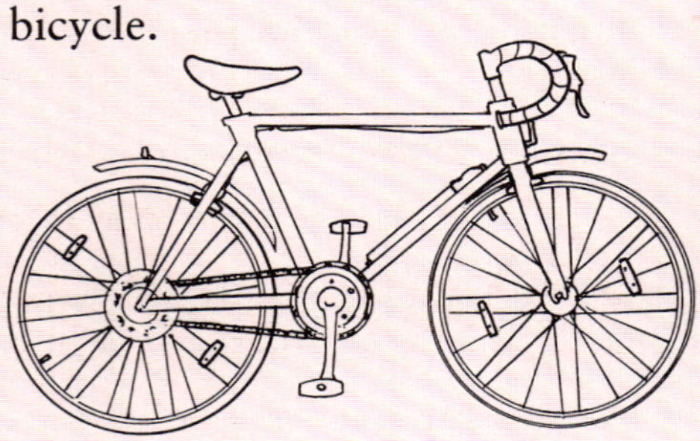

- Mark on the drawing of the bicycle that your teacher has given you all the places where friction is helpful.
- Mark all the places where friction needs to be reduced.

You may need to ask for help from someone who knows about bicycles.

2 Why does keeping a bicycle clean and lubricated make it run better and last longer?

~ Ask the family ~

Ask someone at home to help you to research this task.

Choosing the right lubricant for the job is very important.

1 Describe what kind of lubricant you would use for these articles and why:

- A bicycle chain
- The axle of bicycle
- A car engine
- A sewing machine

You can use brand names if you want but try to describe the appearance and properties of the lubricant if you can.

2 Can you think of a completely different method of reducing friction? (Hint: think of roller-skate wheels.)

DON'T BE CON-FUSED

Homework Activity

1 Find out where the fuse for an electrical appliance is placed in the circuit. Sort the electrical appliances in your home by the type of fuse they need.

HAZARD WARNING: *You will need to ask permission. Make sure anything you handle is unplugged.*

Use a table like the one below to record the size of the fuses needed for different electrical appliances.

3 AMP FUSES	13 AMP FUSES	30 AMP FUSES

~ Ask the family ~

Ask someone at home to help you to research these tasks.

1 Look at some (unplugged or switched off) electrical appliances in your home to find their power rating. This is written in watts or kilowatts (1000 watts = 1 kilowatt).

2 Sort them into three groups according to how much electrical power they use. Decide for yourself how you group them, but explain your reasons clearly.

Aims:

~To understand why electrical fuses are used~

~To understand that different electrical appliances have different power ratings~

National Curriculum:

~Sc4 Physical processes 1f: Currents in circuits~

Background:

~There is more than one way to measure electricity. Each method has its own use.~

~Amps are used for measuring the rating of fuses.~

~Watts are used for measuring how quickly an appliance uses up electrical energy.~

'COOL MAGNET' MYSTERY

Aims:

~To understand that a magnet, and a metal that can be magnetised, will experience a force in the presence of another magnet~

~To identify materials around the home that are magnetic~

National Curriculum:

~Sc4 Physical processes 1g: Magnetic fields~

Homework Activity

You will need two magnets for these experiments. Fridge magnets will do very well if you have any, or you can ask a friend or neighbour to borrow theirs.

1 a) Bring the two magnets close together with the sides that stick onto the fridge facing each other.

b) What happens when you bring the magnets close together? Can you feel a force?

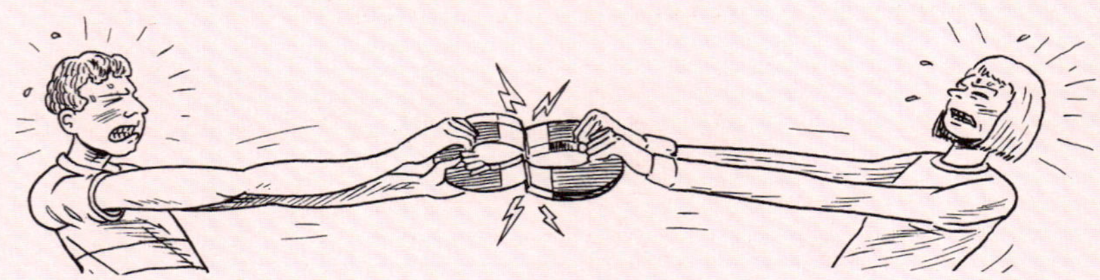

c) Bring them as close together as you can without touching. Now slowly turn one of the magnets around. What happens?

d) Is it easier to hold the magnets apart when they are close together or when they are far away?

Next, you will be investigating what objects, apart from the fridge, your magnets can stick to. First you need to design a table for your results.

2 a) Try sticking your magnet onto ten different things, such as the sink, a pipe or a ring. Write the names of the objects into the correct column of your table.

b) What do you notice about the materials that the magnet stuck to? These are magnetic materials.

c) Did your magnet stick to all the metal objects that you tried?

'COOL MAGNET' MYSTERY

~ Ask the family ~

1 Explain to someone at home (perhaps the person you borrowed the fridge magnets from) what you have found out about magnets.

2 Together, see if you can solve the 'cool magnet' mystery.

A fridge magnet designer has made a magnet called 'cool magnet' that will stick on your fridge *and* *on the cupboard doors in your kitchen. It doesn't use anything sticky and will not leave a mess when you take it off. Cool!*

How do these magnets work? (Clue: On the box that the magnets are sold in it says "cool magnets always come in pairs!")

3 When you think you have worked out the answer, try to reply to some customer queries:

Ms Harris: *I think my 'cool magnet' is wicked! But why doesn't it work on a thick wooden door?*

Mr McDonald: *I've tried making my own 'cool magnet' from ordinary fridge magnets. Why don't they work?*

Ms Tang: *I've had lots of fun with my 'cool magnet'. What I would like to know is why it sometimes falls off after I've turned it?*

Ms Tang's question is tricky. You may need to do some research from a book or a CD ROM.

Background:

~If two magnets are brought close together they will be attracted (move together) or repelled (move apart).~

~One end of a bar magnet will attract and the other end will repel.~

~There is an invisible force between two magnets. The closer the magnets are, the stronger this force will be. The area around a magnet where this force can reach is called its magnetic field.~

~Some metals, such as iron and steel, are affected by magnetic fields. These metals are said to be 'magnetic'.~

SECRETIVE ELECTROMAGNETS!

Aims:

~To research the hiding places of electromagnets in machines in your home~

~To find out where solenoids (electromagnets) are hidden in cars~

National Curriculum:

~Sc4 Physical processes 1j: Electromagnets~

Background:

Here are some clues to help you in this research:

~Your home contains electromagnets hiding inside many everyday things.~

~Many of them also contain an ordinary permanent magnet.~

Homework Activity

1 Use a science textbook or CD ROM to find out which things in your home contain electromagnets. Be warned, there may be more than you think!

2 Draw a cartoon showing all the places where electromagnets lurk unseen.

- Make it funny but informative.
- Add little notes to your cartoon to show where the magnets are.

Draw the inside of one object in detail to reveal its hidden electromagnet.

Never open any appliance plugged into mains electricity. Always ask for permission to look inside an appliance.

3 Why is it important to know where magnets may be hiding?

~ Ask the family ~

Ask someone at home to help you to research this task. You may need to find someone who knows about cars, or even visit a local garage or motor repair shop. If you do, remember to tell someone where you are going, and go with a friend.

- Find out where electromagnets (or solenoids) are used in cars.
- Write an article for a school science magazine called the 'The secret life of electromagnets'.

Homework Activity - Ask the family

You must ask an adult to do this experiment with you. You will need a stop-watch.

1 You are going to measure the speed of cars travelling down a road near your home.

- Find a straight section of road 100 or 200 metres long by pacing out your distance and measuring your paces with a measuring tape.
- You stand at one end and your helper stands at the other end of the measured length of road. The person with the stop-watch should be where the cars pass first. They start their watch when the car passes them and stop it when the car passes the other person. The other person gives a signal when the car goes by.

Ask someone at home to help you to research this task.

2 Find out the current world speed records for the following:

- **land vehicle or car**
- **water vehicle or boat**
- **aircraft travelling in the atmosphere (air)**
- **an animal**
- **a human being**

Aims:

~To work out the speed of cars travelling along the road~

~To research world speed records~

National Curriculum:

~Sc4 Physical processes 2a: Force and linear motion~

Background:

~The speed of anything that is moving can be worked out from two measurements:
a) the distance it travelled, and b) the time it took to travel this distance.~

~Divide the distance by the time.

SPEED = DISTANCE ÷ TIME

~For example, if a car travels 100 km in 2 hours, its speed is 100 ÷ 2, which is 50 km per hour.~

BODIES, REST AND MOTION

Aims:

~*To understand forces by thinking about different sports*~

~*To understand how a car is designed to reduce the effect of forces in a crash*~

National Curriculum:

~*Sc4 Physical processes 2c: Force and linear motion*~

Homework Activity

1 a) Describe how the following things might change when you hit a tennis ball:

- the **shape** of the ball
- the **direction** of the ball
- the **speed** of the ball

b) Find out what 'unbalanced forces' means. Use this phrase to explain why the tennis ball changes in the three ways that you have described.

c) Can you think of any sports that do not involve unbalanced forces?

2 a) Use the words below to describe what happens to a parachutist: i) in free-fall; ii) opening the parachute; iii) hitting the ground.

- **weight** • **balanced forces** • **decelerate**
- **air resistance** • **unbalanced forces** • **accelerate**

Use a diagram to help you.

b) Compare what happens to the parachutist with what happens to a bungee-jumper. How do their experiences differ?

~ Ask the family ~

Ask someone who has a car to help you with the following questions.

1 What protects a car from bumps? What happens to these parts during a crash?

2 Find out what a 'crumple zone' is. How does it protect a person in a car crash?

3 Some new cars have a Side Impact Protection System (SIPS for short). How does SIPS work? Do you think this is a good idea?

4 The above features are designed to squash and bend during a car crash. Why is this useful?

5 Can you think of a feature inside the car which is designed to 'squash' during a crash? In many cars this feature is only for the driver. Why is this? Why don't the other passengers need it?

6 Design a safety leaflet, or a poster, for a car. In your leaflet or poster describe the features of a car that help to protect us. Explain how each one works.

Background:

~If the forces acting upon an object are not equal we say the forces are 'unbalanced'.~

~Unbalanced forces affect either the speed, the shape or the direction of a moving object, or a combination of these things.~

THAT SINKING FEELING

Aims:

~To investigate the 'weight' of objects in air and water, and to explain the results~

~To find out about the Plimsoll line and how ships float~

National Curriculum:

~Sc4 Physical processes 2a: Force and linear motion~

Background:

~Weight is the force due to the pull of the Earth on objects. It is measured, like all forces, in newtons (N for short).~

~1 kg has a gravitational force of roughly 10 newtons. You can change kg to newtons by multiplying by 10.~

Homework Activity

You will need to borrow a hang-up weighing machine used for fishing to do this.

1 Collect some small things that float and some that sink (floaters and sinkers). Attach a piece of cotton to each so that you can hang it on the scale. Look for as many different materials as you can find – metal washers, wood, buttons, even vegetable peelings or fruit.

2 First weigh each object in the air. Then weigh it again with the object hanging in water.

3 Record your results in a table. What do you notice? Is there any difference between the results for floaters and sinkers?

~ Ask the family ~

Ask someone at home to help you to research these tasks.

1 The Plimsoll line is a line marked on the side of ships. Find out what it does.

2 What happens to a ship travelling down a big river when it goes from fresh water into sea water? (The Plimsoll line should give you a clue.)

3 The Dead Sea is very, very salty. How would you expect a ship to float in the Dead Sea compared with ordinary sea water?

A LOAD OFF YOUR MIND!

Homework Activity

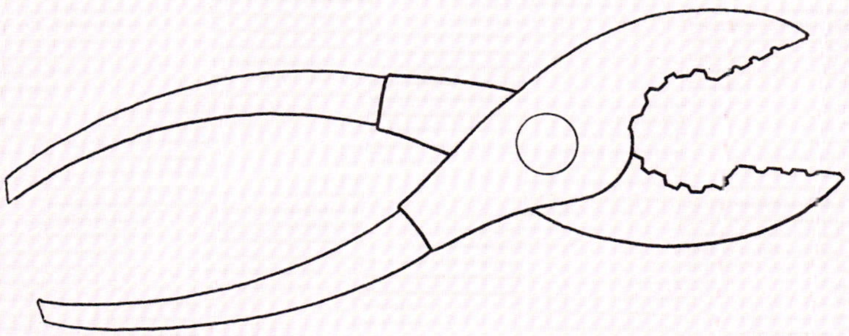

1 How many levers can you see in this picture?

The force produced (load) by a lever is often bigger than the force you make on the on the handle (effort). A tool that does this is called a **force magnifier.**

Levers can also make something move further. The long hand of a clock makes the tiny turn at the centre seem much bigger. These levers are called **distance magnifiers.**

2 Explain the way in which levers work to someone at home. Take your time and help them by showing some examples in the home.

~ Ask the family ~

1 Together with someone at home, collect some tools and other items around your home, garden or garage that are levers or have levers in them.

2 Draw sketches of your levers and mark the pivot, effort and load on each sketch.

3 Decide together which of your tools is a distance magnifier and which is a force magnifier.

Aims:

~To explain to someone at home what you have learned about levers~

~To learn how to recognise levers at home and discover how they are used~

National Curriculum:

~Sc4 Physical processes 2f: Forces and rotation~

Background:

~Many simple machines contain a pivot or turning point. A pivot or turning point is the crucial part of a lever.~

~Levers help to make forces work in a particular direction. They can also make a force larger, or 'magnify' it.~

~Levers have been used by humans for thousands of years.~

~In the diagram on this page, look at the effort (the force you use), the pivot (turning point) and the load.~

DASHING THROUGH THE SNOW

Aims:

~To solve a problem and rescue your school-friends by applying a lesson you have learned in science~

~To use your knowledge of pressure to explain how a variety of winter sports equipment works~

National Curriculum:

~Sc4 Physical processes 2i: Force and pressure~

Homework Activity

1 Your school tennis team is on its way home from a tournament in Italy, but the coach has broken down in a small village high in the Alps. The driver is lost and it's a long way back to the main road. There has been a heavy fall of deep fresh snow and the telephone lines are broken.

You begin to walk back to the main road, but the snow is too deep for walking …

Then you have a brilliant idea. You remember a very useful and more than usually wonderful science lesson about pressure.

Complete this story with your brilliant idea for getting the tennis team back to the hotel!

2 You will need some centimetre squared paper for this task.

The average weight of a member of the tennis team is 50 newtons.

By an amazing coincidence, everyone's shoe size is the same as yours.

a) Use the squared paper to measure the area of your shoe soles.

b) Calculate the pressure each tennis team member would make on the snow wearing shoes.

c) Calculate the pressure each member would make using your brilliant plan. (You will need to measure something else to do this.)

DASHING THROUGH THE SNOW

~ Ask the family ~

Ask someone at home to help you to research these tasks.

In Britain many people enjoy walking in the hills and mountains, even in the winter. For safety on steep ground they often wear crampons on their feet and carry an ice axe.

In Northern Europe and parts of Canada, the ground is covered with deep snow for many months in the winter. People who live there often use skis to visit their neighbours and friends. Children learn to ski when they are very young, and may even go to school on their skis.

1. Find out what crampons, ice axes and skis are and how they work. Most outdoor shops have leaflets and catalogues and would be helpful if you asked.

2. Try to explain how these pieces of equipment work using your understanding of pressure.

Background:

~Pressure is calculated by dividing the force or weight in newtons by the area the force is pressing on.~

~If you press your thumb on a wooden bench your thumb doesn't go into the bench, but if you put a drawing pin under your thumb the pin will go in.~

~The area of your thumb is much bigger than the area of the point of the pin, so all the force from your thumb is passed to the tiny point of the pin.~

~The same principle also works in reverse. Pressure can be reduced by spreading it over a larger area.~

THUNDER AND LIGHT ...

Aims:

~To apply the science of sound and light to common events~

~To research some facts about the universe that are associated with the speed of light~

National Curriculum:

~Sc4 Physical processes 3a: The behaviour of light~

Background:

~Some of the observations in this activity have only recently been made. Some of the explanations are therefore theories or hypotheses.~

~A theory or hypothesis is a way of explaining something we may not fully understand by combining what we know with what we observe.~

Homework Activity

1 Explain the following facts:

a) You can see the lightning before you hear the thunder.

b) Every three seconds you can count between seeing lightning and hearing thunder represents 1 kilometre between you and the storm.

c) The time-keepers of a race start their stop-watches when they see the smoke from the starting pistol, not when they hear the shot.

2 Many science fiction stories have space ships travelling at the speed of light.

Write your own short story about a future time when speed-of-light travel is possible. Make it scientific by including facts such as the speed of light and the distance to the stars. Remember that it would take just over four years to reach the next nearest star at the speed of light.

~ Ask the family ~

Ask someone at home to help you to research these questions.

1 Some stars that we see in the night sky are probably no longer there. How can this be?

2 Why are black holes black?

3 What is the energy source of our own star, the Sun?

SHADOWS IN THE NIGHT

Homework Activity - Ask the family

This investigation will be easier if someone at home helps you. You will need cardboard and a piece of graph paper.

1 Draw a person on the cardboard, cut it out and measure its height.

2 Put the shape in front of a lamp or torch so that it makes a shadow on a wall.

3 Move your shape different distances from the lamp. Write these distances down.

4 What happens to the size of the shadow when you move it? Write the size of the shadow next to each of the distances from the lamp.

5 Draw a graph of your two sets of measurements.

6 What does this graph show? Can you explain this?

7 Find out what sundials are, how they work, and when and where they were first used.

8 Try to find a sundial and copy its face. Can you explain the arrangement of the lines on the face of the sundial?

Aims:

~To investigate how the distance from a light affects shadows~

~To understand what shadows tell you about light~

~To explore how sundials work~

National Curriculum:

~Sc4 Physical processes 3b: The behaviour of light~

Background:

~We are so used to seeing shadows that we hardly ever think about them.~

~Shadows are caused by interrupting light rays.~

~Observing shadows can show us how light travels in straight lines.~

~Sunlight comes from a different direction from morning to evening, and at a different height according to the season.~

WHO IS THE FAIREST OF THEM ALL?

Aims:

~To find and describe the image in a range of mirror types~

~To research uses of mirrors and how they 'fool' our eyes~

National Curriculum:

~Sc4 Physical processes 3e: The behaviour of light~

Background:

~Mirrors can be flat (plane), curved inwards (concave) or curved outwards (convex).~

~Each shape gives a different picture (or image) when you look into it. Different shapes have different uses.~

Homework Activity

1 Find as many mirrors and reflectors as you can. Look in your home, in town and in cars. Some can be found in surprising places, such as torches and electric fires.

Describe the image(s) you can see when you look in each one. Use the following words to help you:

- **Same size**
- **bigger**
- **smaller**
- **upside-down**
- **upright**
- **wide-angle**
- **back-to-front**
- **squashed**
- **stretched**

2 An enlightening poster!

Design a poster for young children about the different mirrors you found. Explain what the different images are like and why. Use the words in question 1 to help you. Draw the different images they make. Explain how each mirror suits its job. Make it bold, funny and easy to understand.

~ Ask the family ~

Ask someone at home to help you to research these questions.

1 Human babies and some animals think they see another baby or animal in front of them when they look at an ordinary mirror. Can you suggest why?

2 Find out about some tricks or special effects that can be done with mirrors.

3 Explain how a mirror makes an image or picture.

SEEING THINGS CLEARLY

Homework Activity

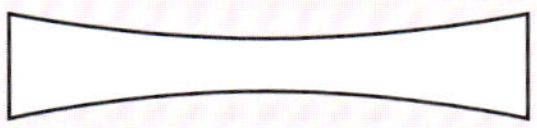

A concave lens

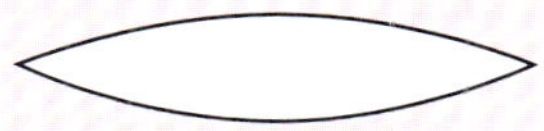

A convex lens

The pictures above show a 'slice' through two kinds of lens.

1 a) Look at a spoon in a glass of water. What optical illusion do you see?

b) Describe carefully what is happening to the light as it leaves the spoon, passes from the water to the air, and travels to your eyes.

2 a) Study the diagram below and draw where a heron hunting fish would see the fish under the water.

b) How do you think the heron manages to catch any fish?

~ Ask the family ~

Ask someone at home to help you with this task. You will need a large sheet of poster paper, a glue stick and some coloured pens.

1 Cut out pictures of devices that contain lenses from old magazines or newspapers.

2 Stick your pictures onto the poster paper, allowing some space in between.

3 Write next to each picture:

- what kind of lens it has
- how the lens is focused
- where the image is produced.

Aim:

~To observe and explain optical illusions caused by objects in water seen from outside~

National Curriculum:

~Sc4 Physical processes 3f: The behaviour of light~

Background:

~When light passes from one transparent (see-through) material to another, the light changes direction and seems to bend.~

~Pieces of glass can be shaped to bend light in useful ways, to make objects seem bigger or smaller.~

~A convex lens can magnify objects. A concave lens can make objects appear smaller.~

RAINBOW!

Aim:

~To understand that white light can be split up into a range of colours~

National Curriculum:

~Sc4 Physical processes 3g: The behaviour of light~

Background:

~White light is a mixture of seven colours.~

~White light can be split up into these colours using a prism.~

~The range of colours that make up white light is known as a spectrum.~

Homework Activity

1 a) Name the seven colours that make up white light.

b) What equipment would you use to split white light up into these colours?

2 Using the words below explain how white light can be split up into seven colours.

- **dispersion**
- **spectrum**
- **refraction**
- **prism**

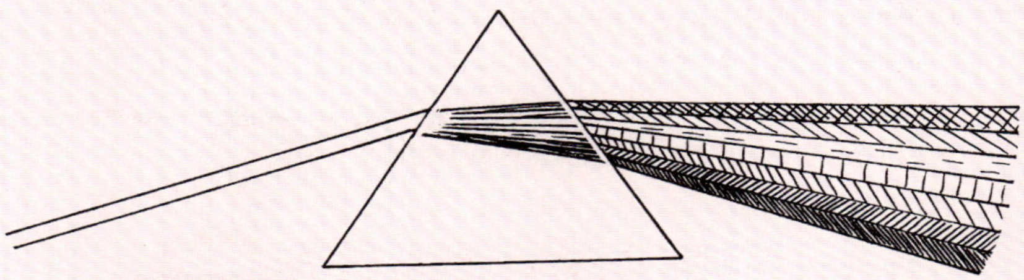

~ Ask the family ~

Explain to someone at home what you know about white light. Together answer the following questions:

1 A rainbow is often seen in the sky. The rainbow contains a spectrum of colours, but how does a rainbow form? What splits sunlight up into the seven colours that we can see?

2 What colour is at the top of a rainbow? Do the colours in a rainbow always appear in the same order?

3 Make a poster showing how rainbows form. Draw a rainbow on your poster, showing the correct colours in the correct order.

DID YOU HEAR THAT?

Homework Activity

1 a) Find out what range of frequencies humans can hear.

b) What happens to our range of hearing as we grow older?

2 a) Draw a line in your science book to show the upper and lower limits of human hearing. Divide the line up to show the normal range of hearing for a human.

b) Find out the frequencies of common sounds, such as voices, cars and aeroplanes. Mark them on your line at the appropriate place. (This is difficult. Don't worry if you can't find them.)

~ Ask the family ~

Explain to someone at home about the hearing range of humans. Ask them to help you with the following questions about the hearing ranges of other animals:

1 Find out which animals can hear sounds that we cannot.

2 Explain how some animals use sounds that humans can't hear, e.g. bats and whales.

3 Find out how bats use sound in order to navigate at night. Why can't we hear most of the sounds bats make?

4 The 'fringed-lipped' bat of South America eats frogs. One problem it faces is that some frogs are poisonous. It knows which frogs to eat because it recognises the croak of an edible frog. What does this tell you about the audible range of this bat compared to humans?

Aim:

~To understand that animals, including humans, have different hearing ranges~

National Curriculum:

~Sc4 Physical Processes 3j: Hearing~

Background:

~Humans can only hear sounds within a certain range of frequencies.~

~The same is also true for other animals.~

TURN IT DOWN!

Aim:

~To know about the effects of loud sounds on the ear~

National Curriculum:

~Sc4 Physical processes 3k: Hearing~

Homework Activity

1 Design an information leaflet about looking after your ears. Your leaflet should:

- describe how the ear works;
- list the different ways in which ears can become damaged;
- explain how to look after your ears and protect them from loud noises;
- include pictures to make it look attractive.

2 Find out what the following words or phrases mean:

- middle ear
- ear drum
- ear canal
- cochlea
- semi-circular canals
- nerve

You may wish to draw a diagram to explain their meanings.

TURN IT DOWN!

~ Ask the family ~

1 Show your information leaflet to someone at home.

2 Ask an older member of your family or an elderly neighbour how their hearing has changed as they have grown older.

3 Find out if there are any sounds they find difficult to hear now.

4 Do you know anyone who works in a noisy environment? If so, ask them how they protect their ears from damage. Has their hearing been affected by noise?

5 Many people wear hearing-aids to help them to hear sounds more easily. Find out what a hearing aid actually does to improve their hearing. Are there any problems associated with using a hearing aid?

6 People who cannot hear well find it difficult to communicate using sound. They may speak to each other using sign language. Find out about sign language. Try to learn the sign language alphabet well enough to finger-spell your name.

Background:

~The ear is very sensitive and can be easily damaged.~

~Loud sounds can damage the inside of a person's ear, and can even burst their eardrum.~

~Repeated sound at the same frequency can make a person become deaf to that frequency.~

~Damage to the ear can cause partial or complete deafness.~

Aim:

~To understand that the apparent movement of the sun is caused by the movement of the Earth~

National Curriculum:

~Sc4 Physical processes 4a: The solar system~

Homework Activity

HAZARD WARNING: NEVER LOOK AT THE SUN DIRECTLY – NOT EVEN THROUGH SUNGLASSES.

1 a) Describe the apparent movement of the Sun during the day. Where does the Sun rise? Where does it set? Where is the Sun at midday?

b) What difference does the time of year (season) make to the way the sun 'moves'? Why does this happen?

2 a) Find out if the way the Sun appears to travel across the sky is the same in different parts of the world. Does the Sun always rise in the East and set in the West? Is there a place where the Sun is always directly overhead at midday?

b) Draw a diagram to show how the Earth travels around the Sun. Show on your diagram where the Earth will be during different seasons.

~ Ask the family ~

1 Show your Sun and Earth diagram to someone at home.

2 Together, try to answer the following questions:

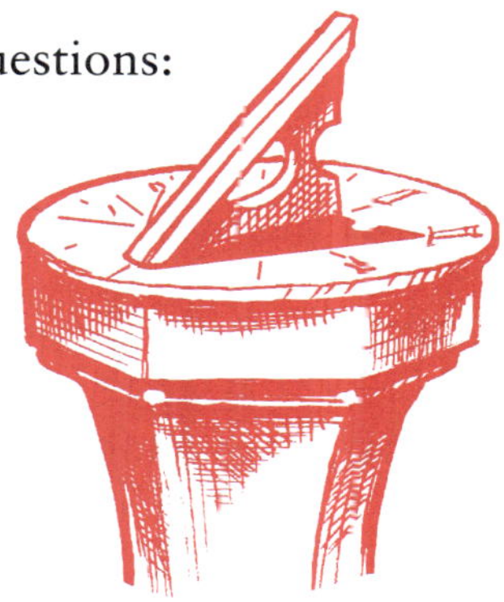

a) Why are shadows shorter in summer than in winter?

b) Why do people who live near the North or South Poles have six dark months each year?

c) Why does the Sun rise in the East and set in the West?

3 Together with someone at home step into your time-machine! Travel back to 1399. The people that you meet believe that the Sun, stars and the planets all travel around the Earth. They think that the Earth doesn't move. Your mission is to prove to them that it is the Earth's movement that causes day and night and the seasons.

4 Write about your visit to 1399. You could explain what happened and how well your mission went in the form of a story, a play or perhaps a letter to a friend. Read it to someone when you've finished.

Background:

~The Sun and the stars appear to move across the sky in daily or yearly cycles.~

~This apparent movement is due to the movement of the Earth.~

~The Earth spins round once in 24 hours. At the same time, it travels round the Sun once in a year.~

THIRD ROCK FROM THE SUN

Aim:

~*To understand the relative positions of the Sun and planets in our solar system*~

National Curriculum:

~*Sc4 Physical processes 4b: The solar system*~

Homework Activity

Answer the following questions in the form of a mini-project or a poster.

1 How far from the Sun is each planet in our solar system?

2 How big is each planet?

3 Which of the planets have one or more moons?

4 How many moons does each planet have?

5 Describe what it might be like to live on another planet. Name the planet and say how hot or cold it is, and how long a day and a year would be.

THIRD ROCK FROM THE SUN

~ Ask the family ~

1 Ask someone at home to help you to find out about space exploration (you may need to find some of the answers from a book or a CD ROM). Show them your project or poster first, and explain to them what you know about the solar system.

2 What do they remember about the moon landings in 1969? Why was this such "a giant leap for mankind"?

3 What were the 'Voyager space missions'? What were scientists trying to find out?

4 In 1997, NASA sent a space vehicle to Mars. What was the vehicle called? Why was NASA so interested in Mars?

5 Write a story about a mission to another solar system. On what kind of planet might you find alien life? Read your story to someone when you have finished.

Background:

~Our solar system consists of a star (the Sun) and nine planets.~

~The planets move around the Sun in a regular and predictable way.~

~Each planet moves in a roughly circular orbit.~

FALLING THROUGH SPACE

Aim:

~To understand that gravity determines how the planets move around the Sun~

National Curriculum:

~Sc4 Physical processes 4c: The solar system~

Homework Activity

1 a) If you throw a ball up in the air, why doesn't it continue to move up for ever? What is the name of the force that brings it back to Earth?

b) If you tied your ball to a piece of string and whizzed it around your head, what would happen if the string broke?

c) The moon travels around the Earth in much the same way as a ball on a string would move around your head. What holds the moon in place? Why doesn't it shoot off into space?

d) What else travels around the Earth due to its gravity?

2 a) The planets all move in a very regular way. What controls their movement?

b) What does gravity depend upon? Does the size of the planet make any difference?

~ Ask the family ~

1 Explain to someone at home what you know about gravity.

2 Using your ideas about gravity, try to explain the following statements so that your helper understands:

a) At the seaside the sea rises and falls twice a day.

b) Jupiter has 16 moons but Earth only has one.

c) Pluto has no atmosphere.

d) On the Moon you would weigh less than you do on Earth.

e) During a mission to Mars, the astronauts have to swing around Venus first!

3 If you have time, do some research into 'black holes'. Why would it be very dangerous to go near a black hole? What precautions would you have to take? Write a story about your journey to a black hole.

Background:

~Our solar system consists of a star, the Sun, and nine planets.~

~The planets travel round the Sun in a regular and predictable way.~

~The planets move in such a way because the force of gravity holds them in place.~

GREAT BALLS OF FIRE!

Aims:

~To know that the Sun and other stars are sources of light~

~To understand that other objects in space are seen by reflected light~

National Curriculum:

~Sc4 Physical processes 4d: The solar system~

Background:

~Most of the points of light that we see in the night sky come from stars. Stars shine because they give out light, just like our Sun.~

~Some objects in the night sky, such as the Moon, Earth satellites and other planets in the solar system, can only be seen because they reflect light from the Sun.~

Homework Activity

1 a) How does the shape of the Moon appear to change during a period of four weeks?

b) Why does the Moon seem to change like this?

c) How does this help us to explain that the Moon does not produce light?

d) What other objects in the night sky do not produce light? How do we see them?

e) What is the biggest difference between a star like our Sun and a planet such as Earth?

2 a) How do we know that the Sun produces light?

b) What is the scientific word for light bouncing off a surface?

~ Ask the family ~

1 Explain the differences between a star and a planet to someone at home.

2 In 1997, NASA sent a robot buggy to Mars. How did they know that Mars was rocky and not a ball of burning gas like the Sun?

3 Together, discuss why it would be impossible for us to live on Mercury or Pluto without special equipment. What special equipment would we need?

WATCH THIS SPACE

Homework Activity

1 Find out what a satellite is. What satellites does Earth have?

2 Write down some jobs that artificial satellites do.

3 Find out how artificial satellites could explore the solar system.

4 a) Mountaineers sometimes use a device called GPS. Find out what GPS stands for?

b) Why do mountaineers use GPS? Who else might be interested in using GPS?

c) What does 'geostationary' mean?

~ Ask the family ~

1 Discuss artificial satellites with someone at home. Ask them to help you with the following questions.

2 Try to think of ways in which artificial satellites have changed our lives.

3 Find out what the Hubble Space Telescope is used for. Why do you think it is useful to have a telescope in space when there are so many on Earth?

4 Many artificial satellites have been put into orbit around other planets. Can you find out any of their names?

5 Discuss whether it is worth spending a lot of money on exploring the solar system. Depending on what you decide, write an argument for or against space exploration.

Aim:

~To understand that artificial satellites can observe the Earth and explore the solar system~

National Curriculum:

~Sc4 Physical processes 4e: The solar system~

Background:

~Hundreds of artificial satellites orbit the Earth carrying out different jobs.~

~Some satellites watch the Earth's weather and help ships and planes to navigate.~

~Some satellites are used for communications such as TV or telephones.~

~Some satellites are sent to orbit other planets, or our Sun, and send back information about the solar system.~

ENERGETIC STUFF

Aim:

~To understand that there are different sources of energy~

National Curriculum:

~Sc4 Physical processes 5a: Energy resources~

Background:

~Energy is important to all living things.~

~Energy also makes machines work.~

~There are many different sources of energy, such as oil, coal, gas, wind, batteries, sunlight and food.~

Homework Activity

1 Design a poster showing all the different sources of energy you can think of. Include a picture of each energy source and write a short paragraph about it.

2 Using your knowledge of energy resources, name the source of energy used by each of the following things:

- **a portable computer**
- **a car**
- **a clockwork toy**
- **a green plant**
- **a steam engine**
- **a sailing ship**
- **a solar powered calculator**
- **YOU**

~ Ask the family ~

1 Ask someone at home to help you to explain which energy resource would be most appropriate for the following situations:

a) *Lisa lives on an island off the coast of Scotland. It is very windy and the waves are often very large.*

b) *Alex and Nadia visit an isolated village in Yemen. The villagers keep lots of cattle. How could the cattle help them to make heat energy for cooking?*

c) *Philip lives in a tiny village in Africa. He has very few cattle and no electricity. What type of energy resource is readily available to him?*

Homework Activity

For this activity you will need to do some research from a book or a CD ROM.

1 Carry out a mini-project on energy resources. Concentrate on where the energy comes from or how it is produced. For example, for fossil fuels you will need to find out how coal, oil and gas are made; for wind energy you will need to find out what makes the wind blow.

Present your project as a poster, essay, pamphlet or spider diagram. If you have a video camera you could even present your information like a TV science programme.

~ Ask the family ~

1 Show your project on energy resources to someone at home.

2 Now work out how the Sun is involved in the creation of each energy resource.

3 If the Earth's atmosphere became thick with dust, the Sun could no longer shine through the clouds. What might this do to energy resources on Earth?

4 Try to find out how long our present energy reserves are expected to last?

5 How could we use up our energy resources more slowly?

6 Imagine that you are advising the government about energy. Make a list of ways to save energy.

Aim:

~To understand that the Sun is the original source of most energy resources on Earth~

National Curriculum:

~Sc4 Physical processes 5b: Energy resources~

Background:

~There are many different sources of energy on Earth.~

~These include coal, oil, gas, nuclear power, food and wind.~

~Most of these resources originally came from the Sun.~

Aim:

~To understand that electricity can be generated from a variety of energy resources~

National Curriculum:

~Sc4 Physical processes 5c: Energy resources~

Homework Activity – Ask the family

1 Explain to someone at home what each of the keywords on the opposite page means. Together, try to answer the next question.

2 You are an advisor to an expedition which is travelling to an island in the Arctic Ocean. The expedition consists of biologists, chemists and geologists who will be studying wildlife and rocks, both around the coast and in the mountains. You are informed by the explorers of the following expedition details:

- It is so cold on the island that any liquid fuel such as petrol would freeze.
- Geologists report that there may be some coal and peat near the coast where a small group of biologists will be observing birdlife for two weeks.

EXPLORING ELECTRICITY

- There are high mountains in the west of the island where some chemists are interested in the properties of a rare flower. They will need to work there for several weeks.
- The base camp will be set up near a large waterfall and lake, with a source of hot water from deep in the Earth.
- Two geologists plan to visit a cave system in the south of the island. They are interested in studying a rare dinosaur fossil that was found by a previous expedition.

Using some of the key words below, prepare a report for the explorers on how each team of scientists could make electricity for heating, cooking and lighting.

- wind energy
- tidal energy
- solar energy
- geothermal energy
- fossil fuels
- wave energy
- biomass
- hydroelectric energy
- chemical energy (e.g. batteries)

Background:

~Energy is important to all living things.~

~Energy also makes machines work.~

~Many different sources of energy, such as oil, coal, gas, sunlight, wind and batteries can be used to produce electricity.~

EVERLASTING ENERGY?

Aim:

~To understand that some of the Earth's energy resources can be used again and some cannot~

National Curriculum:

~Sc4 Physical processes 5d: Energy resources~

Homework Activity

1 Draw a poster showing all the different types of energy resources you can think of. Split your energy resources into ones that are renewable and ones that are non-renewable. List the advantages and disadvantages of each resource.

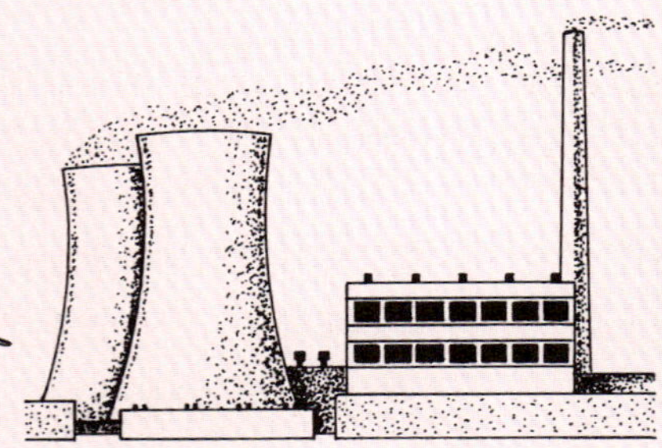

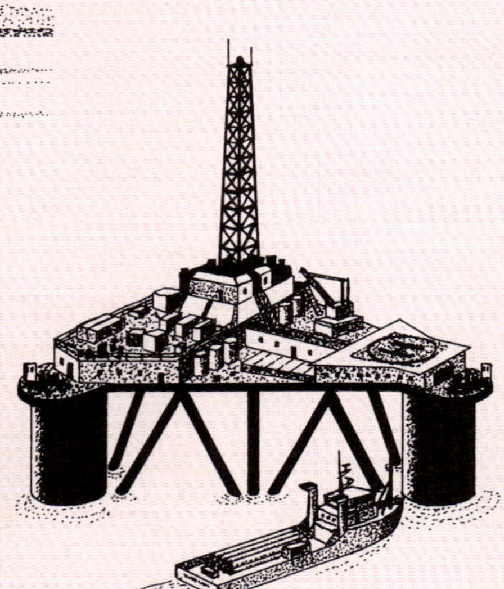

EVERLASTING ENERGY?

~ Ask the family ~

1 Show your poster to someone at home. Ask them to help you with the following questions.

2 Why is it wasteful to use fossil fuels to make electricity?

3 Find out when each type of fossil fuel is expected to run out. Will they run out in your lifetime?

4 How do you think your life would change if fossil fuels ran out tomorrow?

5 Nuclear energy can be used as an alternative to fossil fuels. Why are some people worried about nuclear energy?

6 There are many environmentally friendly energy resources which are renewable. Why do you think that fossil fuels and nuclear power have not already been completely replaced by such fuels?

7 Imagine that you are about to give a speech in Parliament. Decide whether you are for or against nuclear power and fossil fuels. Write down what you would say in favour of your chosen energy resource. What would you say to convince people that other resources are not as good as your own choice?

Background:

~Some of the Earth's energy resources, such as wind and wave energy, can be used again and again.~

~These types of energy are said to be renewable.~

~Energy resources which are destroyed when they are used, such as burning oil or coal, are described as non-renewable.~

Glossary

Acid
A sour-tasting, corrosive solution with a pH of less than 7.

Adapted
How an animal or plant suits where it lives.

Alkali (base)
An alkali is a base that is soluble in water. The opposite of an acid. A corrosive solution with a pH of more than 7.

Artery
A blood tube that carries blood away from the heart. It has thick muscular walls. A pulse can be felt in an artery.

Atoms
The smallest particle in which elements can normally exist.

Bonded
Joined together.

Cancer
A group of diseases. Cells grow out of control, making lumps (tumours). These diseases can kill unless treated quickly.

Capillary
The smallest blood tubes, found in between arteries and veins. They deliver things to and pick up things from the cells.

Cells
All living things are made from tiny parts called cells. Some living things have only one cell in their body, e.g. bacteria. Others have many cells, like humans or oak trees. Groups of cells are called tissues.

Chemical change
New chemicals are produced when a chemical change takes place. The new chemicals have different properties to the ones from which they were made.

Chemical reaction
New chemicals are produced when a chemical reaction takes place. The new chemicals have different properties to the ones from which they were made.

Classifying
Sorting things into useful groups.

Combined
Joined together.

Compete
Have a competition for something, like food, light or a mate.

Compound
Two or more elements joined together.

Condom
A tube of rubber placed over the penis to prevent pregnancy or spreading diseases.

Conductor
A material that carries electricity or heat.

Conductor of electricity
A material that carries electricity.

Conductor of heat
A material that carries heat.

Contract
To shrink or get smaller.

Crystals
Chemicals where the atoms are arranged in a pattern which shows in the shape of the material, e.g. cubes of salt crystals.

Cuttings
Pieces of plants cut off and planted to grow new plants. They have the same genes as the plant they were cut from.

Decompose
Rot or break down, when bacteria or fungi feed on something.

Diet
The foods you eat over a period of time.

Dispersion
Spread out, e.g. a prism spreads out the colours making up white light.

Distilling
Heating liquids with different boiling points to separate a mixture.

Driving limit
The maximum (most) alcohol you can legally drive with in your blood.

Drug
A chemical which changes the way in which the body works. It may change the way you feel or think. It may be a medicine.

Element
A pure substance made of only one type of atom. For example, copper is made of only copper atoms, it is an element.

Energy transfer
When energy is changed from one form to another.

Environment
The surroundings of a living thing.

Enzymes
Special proteins which speed up chemical reactions in living things. They are used in digestion to break down big food molecules into small ones.

Erosion
Small pieces of rock or soil are moved by rivers, streams, the sea or wind.

Evaporate
When a liquid changes into a gas.

Expand
When materials get bigger in size, often when they are heated.

Fair testing
Keeping all the factors (things) the same, apart from the ones you are investigating.

Fertilised
When an egg cell nucleus and a sperm cell nucleus join. Or when a pollen cell nucleus joins with the egg cell nucleus of a flower.

Fertiliser
Chemicals or natural rotting things put into soil to help plants grow.

Filling
A mixture of metal used to plug holes in teeth.

Filter
To separate solids from liquids, or big bits of solid from smaller bits, using a kind of sieve or filter.

Fossil fuels
Fuels taken from rocks, e.g. coal, oil and gas.

Foundations
The base of walls often dug into the ground or under the ground.

Functions
The jobs that parts of living things do.

Illustrated
Pictures or diagrams in your work.

Indicators
Chemicals which change colour to tell you that another chemical is in a mixture, e.g. universal indicator goes red in strong acids.

Indigestion
When you can't digest your food very well. It makes your stomach feel uncomfortable or painful. It can be caused by too much acid being made in your stomach.

Inherited
A feature passed down from one generation to the next.

Invertebrate
An animal without a backbone or skeleton inside its body.

Investigation
Trying to find out something or answer a question by doing an experiment.

Lethal
Can kill you.

Lifestyle
The way you live your life. Your food, the amount of exercise you get, what you spend your time doing.

Lubricant
A chemical like oil that is put on moving parts so they move past one another more easily. It reduces friction.

Magnetic
A material that is attracted by a magnet.

Minerals
Natural compounds found in the Earth's rocks and soils. Most living things need minerals to live healthy lives.

Mixtures
More than one chemical mixed up together, but not joined together.

Molecules
One or more types of atom joined or bonded to another type of atom.

Neutralise
To cancel out. When an acid neutralises an alkali it makes a neutral solution with a pH of 7.

Non-metal
An element which is not a metal!

Nutrition
How a living thing feeds.

Organ
A clear part of a living thing's body, that does a clear job or jobs.

Organic
A chemical that has come from the body of another living thing.

Oxidise
When a substance joins or combines with oxygen, we say it has been oxidised.

Particles
The little bits the make up all the matter or materials in the universe – atoms and molecules.

Passive smoking
When you breathe in someone else's cigarette smoke.

Period
When the lining of the womb comes away and causes bleeding each month.

Physical change
A change in the pattern of the atoms or molecules where no new chemical is made, e.g. melting, freezing, evaporating and condensing.

Pivot
The turning point or fulcrum of a machine.

Pods
The part of a plant that has the seeds inside, like a pea-pod.

Pollution
Chemicals released into the environment which damage living things or the balance of nature in some way.

Pressure
The force of an object divided by the area it is pressing on.

Puberty
Changes in the body and mind of a teenager that prepare them for becoming parents in the future.

Reactivity
How reactive a chemical is. How ready it is to react with other chemicals.

Recycled
Re-using chemicals or materials, not wasting them.

Refraction
When light passes from one transparent (see-through) material to another the light changes direction and seems to 'bend'.

Respiration
The release of energy from food inside cells. Oxygen is needed to do this.

Revision
Learning ideas carefully by reading, taking notes and answering questions.

Rock cycle
How types of rock on earth are recycled over millions of years.

Safari
Travelling to observe animals in their natural habitat.

Selective breeding
Breeding animals or plants to produce features you want, like taste in apples or thick wool in sheep.

Sexual reproduction
Producing young animals or plants by sperm and eggs (or pollen and eggs) joining together.

Solute
The solid that dissolves in a liquid to make a solution.

Solution
When a solid (or sometimes another liquid) dissolves in a liquid to make a solution, e.g. salt in water makes a salt solution.

Solvent
The liquid that dissolves a solid to make a solution.

Spectrum
The range of coloured light that can be produced from white light by passing it through a prism. A rainbow is a spectrum produced by raindrops acting like prisms.

Sperm
Male sex cells in animals that have a tail and swim to the female egg cell.

Symbols
One or two letters are used throughout the world as a shorthand way of writing down each element, e.g. Cu for copper, H for hydrogen, I for iodine.

Territory
An area lived in by an animal that it treats as its own. It defends this territory from other animals.

Texture
How something feels to touch, e.g. how rough, smooth or lumpy something is.

Variation
Differences between living things.

Vein
A blood tube that returns blood to the heart, with thin walls, containing valves.

Vertebrate
An animal with a backbone and a skeleton inside its body.

Weathering
The way that rocks are broken into small pieces by the weather.

Weight
The force of gravity on a thing, measured in newtons.